FOCUSED

# FOCUSED

## THE PREPARED TO WIN MINDSET

# JJ MOSES

**FIDELIS**
BOOKS

A FIDELIS BOOKS BOOK
An Imprint of Post Hill Press
ISBN: 979-8-88845-291-2
ISBN (eBook): 979-8-88845-292-9

Focused:
The Prepared to Win Mindset
© 2023 by JJ Moses
All Rights Reserved

Post Hill Press
New York · Nashville
posthillpress.com

Published in the United States of America

This book is dedicated to my loving
Dad and Mom, Jerry & Shirley Moses—

Your unconditional love and support
is what allowed me to dream BIG!

Also to my parents-in-law,
Ipe and Susie Mathai—

You are an inspiration to me and I'm so
grateful for your love and support.

# CONTENTS

## Level II. Building a Deeper Foundation

## Level III. Forge an Unstoppable Team Culture

# FOREWORD

## BY JOEL OSTEEN

We all face times when we feel that we're at a disadvantage, that we got shortchanged, that the odds are against us and we can never win. It's easy to go through life thinking of all the reasons why we can't be successful. "I'm the underdog here. I'm not talented enough, strong enough, or smart enough. Others have more experience, more qualifications, more resources, and they get the good breaks, the best positions. If I had a better personality, if I were more confident, if I were more attractive, I could reach my dreams." The problem is that if you stay focused on what you think you don't have, it's going to cause you to shrink back and keep you from rising higher. It's going to limit your life. That's a deficit mentality.

As one of the most inspiring and encouraging people I know, I can think of no one better to write this book on developing a winning mindset than my friend JJ Moses.

JJ had to fight through one barrier after another of being told he was too small to achieve his dream of playing college football or in the NFL. He could have easily been talked out of what God put in his heart, but he refused to let others determine whether or not he could succeed at the highest level. JJ is living proof that God loves to choose the underdog, the least likely, the one others write off and discount, and cause them to break through and be catapulted from the back to the front.

I've known JJ since his playing days with the Houston Texans over twenty years ago, when he electrified fans with his speed as a kickoff and punt returner. He started serving as an usher at our church and has become a great servant leader here. I've watched him overcome overwhelming odds, taking the winning lessons he's learned and turning them into the NFL's number-one professional and personal development program.

JJ's words of practical wisdom, encouragement, and faith on how to approach your life, your career, and your relationships will inspire you as his words have so often inspired me. I urge you to read this book and embrace the insight and encouragement you'll find on every page. If you allow them to take hold and commit yourself to running your race with a winning mindset and positive focus, you will soon step into the power and abundance that God intended you to have and become all you were created to be.

# INTRODUCTION
# THE "PREPARE TO WIN" BLUEPRINT

On September 8, 1978, my parents Jerry and Shirley Moses were taking a car ride and enjoying a beautiful day in Waterloo, Iowa. Suddenly, the fear of accident and death broke through their serene and peaceful day. As they were about to cross over the railroad tracks, a set of beaming lights came into full view from the side, heading directly toward them. No crossing signs illuminated, and they were hit by over one hundred tons of steel traveling at over forty miles per hour. The train dragged their car, with them inside, for nearly fifty feet. When everything came to a standstill, they both miraculously walked away without a scratch.

One year from the date of the accident—on September 8, 1979—they were expecting the arrival of their first child. As the due date passed, the doctors discovered that the baby's heartbeat was growing faint and that a C-section was necessary to ensure survival. Well, I may have been a few days late, but I finally arrived on September 12, 1979, as a healthy nine-pound boy, ready to meet the world.

It's no coincidence that my parents were in an accident but walked away without a scratch. It's no coincidence that a year to the date of the accident I was expected to arrive. It's no coincidence that, despite my faint heartbeat, I arrived healthy and full of life. Because, despite the challenges, there was a plan in place for my parents and for my life. I believe you are also reading this book because of a plan.

There is a saying that goes, "In school you are taught a lesson, then given a test. In life you are given the test to teach you a lesson." There are times in life when situations can be messy, things do not add up, or you put in the hard work but do not have anything to show for it.

I'm reminded of a gala my wife and I attended years ago where a painter created art right in front of us. When the painter began to work on the painting, he started with a blank canvas. Then he began to combine colors. He brushed and blended the canvas with various tools. At first it looked a little messy and unformed. As he continued to work, however, the colors and shapes began to come together. Then, with a few final strokes, a masterpiece appeared right before our eyes. In life, things may look uncertain and even unformed at times, but know that your life is being painted by God. He is aware of what is needed to make your life into a beautiful masterpiece.

In sports, each team has a specific game plan that enables them to ultimately win. However, it's also about being able to deal with adversity, not flinching when things get hard, and staying focused on the strategy that leads to championship results. It also takes preparation, which is why I believe winners do not win by chance; they have a sustained mindset that gives them the ultimate advantage. I was blessed to have a career in the National Football League for four seasons, which was an improbable opportunity considering I am 5'6" and did not fit the prototype of an NFL athlete. Statistics showed that I had a 0.2 percent chance of making a roster.

In this book, you will discover the blueprint to the Prepare to Win mindset, which is constructed around three significant levels of proficiency. Once you've started to implement them into your own life, you'll understand how they helped me overcome all the odds of making it into the National Football League. Generally, it's about intentional focus, resiliency, faith, and positivity. It incorporates your emotions, spirituality, and social health and ensures that you develop the skills necessary to achieve what you desire in life.

Your dreams and goals are the ideas, careers, projects, desires, adventures, and solutions you think about constantly. Any one of them can be fueled by the belief that you were created to do something bigger than yourself. They can feel like a set of solutions to a problem in your world. It can be something that feels impossible, but you can't seem to shake it from your thoughts. Your present reality may be the total opposite of what you are dreaming and capable of. In many ways, you might feel like life has become mundane and purposeless. You might find yourself wondering if life will ever change—will it get any better?

If you identify with any of these statements, be encouraged, because I know you can experience a shift in your life by incorporating the principles in this book. It will take faith, effort, commitment, and perseverance, but your dream is waiting for you. Are you ready?

There is an honest saying that goes around locker rooms when you first enter the National Football League: "The NFL stands for 'Not For Long.'" Meaning, you may not have the luxury of a long-term career because you could get cut from the team, or, even worse, an injury could shorten your playing days. This reality hit me—and it came direct from the mouths of veteran players who had experienced the realities of professional football—in a moment when I imagined myself celebrating for having achieved a lifelong goal. I looked around the locker room, and I realized, regardless of the amazing players I was surrounded by, no matter how many records would be set or how fast a player ran the forty-yard dash, there was going to be a time when that saying was going to come true.

This harsh reality was a bit of a shock, but I appreciated it because it brought me into a newfound perspective. Regardless of how often I was on TV sets on Sunday afternoons or how many fans I played in front of, the achievement of playing in the NFL was not going to sustain me for my entire life. I was proud of my focused work to get to that point, but the reinterpreted acronym hammered home a valuable lesson that emphasized winning as something that didn't just refer to sports anymore. Now, to "win" meant attaining the complete life I'd always imagined.

"Not For Long" isn't only locked into the football experience. We all experience a variation of it in our lives no matter what goal we're focused on. Successes will come and go, but we need to construct a stable foundation to absorb the impact of life's blindside hits. Fortunately, I was blessed to have parents who prepared me for situations like entering the Kansas City Chiefs' facility and having that "not for long" locker-room wisdom dropped on me. I was also fortunate to know the importance of embracing a process. I had experienced how they brought structure and strategy to what felt like chaotic situations. When I was a kid, they led me in times of transition, uncertainty, setbacks, and failures. They helped put everything in perspective so I never mistook the NFL for a so-called promised land where I could get comfortable.

My parents helped shaped my mindset where I saw the NFL as a field of perpetual training and preparation instead of the golden ticket to a made life. Every situation I encountered transformed into a lesson that first helped me grow and then became something that I could use to teach, impact, and motivate others to win at life. Whether you are in retail, the government, healthcare, marketing, or real estate, these steps will help you win too.

In high school, I would write the word "focus" all over my notebooks. In art class, I made a chain and a necklace that said "focus." I would get haircuts and have the barber write "focus" in the back of my head. And so, focus was my motto. It was my statement.

When I was in college, during my first couple of years at Iowa State—being in a new town, a new environment, with new friends and a new coaching staff—I found myself in a state of transition, and I had to rediscover that mindset. Sometimes you lose that focus because you're trying to adjust. And that's the situation I found myself in, so I had to go back to my roots, in a manner of speaking. But once I rediscovered that mindset, I noticed an immediate change. I earned a starting position on the football team, which came with great wins and awards, and eventually an NFL contract too. It brought me a new level of influence.

Still, it's not always easy—especially when you're trying to be different or do something that's never been done. Don't be surprised if you feel a sense of alienation. It's one of those things that just won't make sense to everybody. Once, in high school, we were getting ready to play a big game, and I told our team in front of the coaches, "Guys, we need to stay focused. We don't need to be chasing after girls or partying. We need to stay focused on working out and playing great football."

When my teammates heard me say this, they looked around at each other and were like, "Man, what are you talking about? What are you talking about not chasing after girls or going out to have fun? Man, you trippin'!"

But looking back, there was a realization of the level of my intention and focus.

The focused mindset won't make sense to everybody. At least not in the moment. It can make people feel uncomfortable. But sooner or later they will always come back around full circle and say, "Ah, wow, I understand why you were like that."

This book is written to help you transform your day-to-day mindset so that you too can start performing up to your potential. Remember, however, that certain habits will take patience and practice to form, which is why the book is constructed in levels and steps. Try to avoid implementing them all at once. Just take them one at a time—at your own pace—and you'll be prepared to win before you know it.

# LEVEL 1

## SETTING A HIGHER STANDARD

To achieve a winning mindset, you first need to ensure that all aspects of your life are working together toward a common purpose. This includes aligning your values, beliefs, and actions with your career, relationships, health, and personal development. When you are holistically aligned, you feel a sense of harmony, balance, and satisfaction. You are conscious of the choices you make and how they affect your overall well-being. You're in tune with your body, mind, and soul. You're being true to yourself, and not compromising on your values and beliefs for the sake of external validation or societal expectations. By being holistically aligned, you are able to live life with intention, authenticity, and fulfillment.

Your internal sense of self will match your external reputation.

I have been around all types of social classes, from the wealthy to those struggling to pay rent. From a distance, wealth can create the illusion of problem-free glamour; the realization hits that it is hollow if you don't have a good name. My parents instilled in me that a person's reputation is far more important than the material things society encourages us to focus on.

The financial world works on grading you, even branding you with a "score" that alerts other money institutions what your reputation is. But much more powerful and meaningful is the score your peers give you in life. Before you even enter a room, your reputation precedes you. As you'll see, I learned firsthand how a good reputation opens doors. A poor reputation, on the other hand, limits your potential and experiences. By extension, your score wears off on friends and business partners, or whomever you choose to associate with. Likewise, their reputation reflects on you and either helps build or detract from yours.

After I graduated from high school, I was preparing to go to college. That summer, the manager at my mother's workplace offered me a full-time job—the kind that had the potential to turn into a career. I decided to focus on college, but my appreciation for the offer was directly related to realizing why I had been offered it in the first place—my parents' reputation. The manager knew my parents' "score," their reputation, which in turn benefitted me.

It takes a lifetime to build up your reputation, but just seconds to destroy it. My parents took on the job of molding our character and used our shared experiences to illustrate how quickly hard work can be neutralized. While they never referred to it as such, holistic alignment was what they ultimately emphasized by setting a higher standard for ourselves and our lives. They knew how integral internal harmony was to external acceptance, performance, and, ultimately, success.

It's vital to always be aware of your internal and external narratives, and of where they differ and align. We live in a time where people talk about building a brand, getting more followers, and being influential, but the most powerful way to achieve goals and influence is to build yourself from the inside out—mentally, spiritually, physically, and emotionally. When you are holistically aligned, when all the aspects of yourself are in order, then you will feel guided as you enter unfamiliar circumstances.

What do others think of you when they hear your name?

# STEP 1.

# PUT YOUR GOALS WHERE YOU CAN SEE THEM

A study conducted by Harvard Business School suggested that only 3 percent of their students wrote down their goals; 13 percent had clearly defined goals but did not write them down. The remaining 84 percent were unable to identify a specific goal. Ten years later, the study circled back and looked at the participants. The 13 percent who had clearly defined goals but didn't write them down were making, on average, twice as much as the participants who couldn't state their goals. What really got my attention, however, was the 3 percent who had clearly defined goals and wrote them down. They earned as much as ten times more than the rest of the unwritten group put together.

As you can see, this exercise is vital, and a lot more difficult than you might imagine (if you're a person who has yet to write down their aspirations). You might have a floating thought in your head—existing in a realm of shorthand self-talk—and you might think that you fully understand it. But try to explain it to somebody else, and you can easily see how muddled and tangled it can become. If you write it down, all the mental shortcuts that you create fall apart, and you are forced to break down the process of achieving your goal in clearly defined language, of the kind that will be understandable for anybody.

A lot of studying is done in the NFL. Some of it is conscious, and some happens so fast that it doesn't register until you look back and see how you processed the information. I would be running as fast as I could and see holes or catch a glimpse of how a linebacker angled his foot and I'd already be veering away from the direction I knew he was pivoting toward. But one thing I always noticed as I was looking for an advantage to exploit on the field was the defenders' positioning, footwork, and eyes. The elite players specially noticed these small indicators to help them make a decision. Elite players had an ability to put their entire concentration into a single point of focus, even as I was doing my best to confuse them.

I see the same thing when I look at a world-class sprinter or pro basketball player—their eyes are fixed ahead on the target as they run or shoot the ball. As a kick returner, I spent the majority of my NFL career zeroing in on an oblong pigskin-covered object flying through the air. If my concentration broke, then any number of things could go wrong. My hands wouldn't be ready to catch the ball at the precise moment, or it would bounce off my chest, or I might misjudge the distance and have to lunge forward to make an off-balance catch. Just like in life, there are a million ways to fumble on any given play.

So, I learned how to block out the static. As a pro football player, you need to learn how to block out the flashes of the cameras, the tens of thousands of fans—cheering or taunting—the millions of people watching on TV and make it all evaporate with your focus. But if you focus on the wrong thing? Bask in the warmth of fans chanting your name or cheering you on? That can dilute the focus you have available for what matters. When you get it right though, the most beautiful moments can unfold. Time and distractions fall away, and a kind of creativity takes over, allowing you to actualize your potential.

Sometimes this focus is so inherent to high achievers that they have trouble translating it into words for others as a lesson. I'd sit around rooms with players who had attained what most athletes only dream of. But reaching your dreams is not a one-stop ride. I saw too many exceptional athletes make the squad and then flounder, unable to maintain the motivation necessary to perform at an elite level. After I was done playing, it became my job to provide a structure for their focus.

One of the most powerful tools I have used is one that usually elicits murmurs around a meeting table. What I do is place a piece of paper and a pen in front of each chair, and when the team meeting starts, I instruct everyone to write their goals out—physically—on paper.

I've had business professionals who make jaw-dropping presentations and players who can memorize hundreds of complicated plays struggle mightily with this—it isn't easy, but that is what makes it so valuable. Writing something down imprints it on our souls in a much more meaningful way than just saying it out loud. There is power in the pen—which is why I've become intentional about physically recording my thoughts, goals, aspirations, prayers—anything I truly hope to accomplish. Like a lot of the administrators and players I have worked with, you might feel reluctant at the start, but when you do it enough, you will be blown away by how the simple process of writing jumpstarts the process of taking action.

Writing down goals is proven to make a more indelible imprint on you as a person, but I also want to encourage you to post your written aspirations in a place where you see them throughout the day. Just glimpsing them paves a neuropathway in your brain. I use prayer in the same manner—put up on the wall as a constant reminder to meditate on it when I'd otherwise be thinking about what's for dinner or if it's time to rotate the tires. But more than that, I also appreciate the reminder I have given myself—it can feel like a gift to pause and make sure I am on the right path.

And, as anybody who has written a grocery list or a to-do list knows—does it ever *not* feel good to cross something off your list?

When I work with student athletes, so many of them tell me how they dream of playing in the NFL or NBA and, of course, I tell them to look at me—5′6″ and undrafted, and I made it. How? I tell them to start right now with something they can all do immediately—write that goal down! Pin it up on the wall! Modify it and meditate on it and refine it with smaller goals to build on. Maybe you want to start your NBA journey by building up to sinking seventy free throws out of a hundred—write it down! Beat a hundred-yard dash personal time? Write it down and put a check next to it when you achieve that goal. You'll find that you create more and more mini goals, and there is no more sure pathway to achieving major goals than by focusing on the details first.

I started writing down my goals when I was in high school, and when I say started, I mean with typical teenager energy. Holy smokes—I hung up so much paper that it technically could have been wallpapering! But I LOVED looking at those messages to myself. There was so much that I wanted to accomplish, and the goals reminded me of my potential. I still had to work hard to achieve my dreams, but seeing the notes made me realize that it was up to me to meet the challenges. When you see a note that you wrote to *yourself*, it becomes difficult to make up an excuse for not pursuing it.

I learned to create a goals system and would prioritize them so that when I accomplished one, I was able to move on to the next. Some I got stuck on, and it took a frustratingly long time to check them off, but often what I learned from the struggle made the next hurdle that much easier to clear.

I've become motivated with how effective this simple act is and how it changes lives. Whenever I have speaking engagements, there is a point where I ask the audience how many of them write their goals down. It's always close to the same percentage of that Harvard Business Study group. Maybe 20 percent of the people raise their hands.

I take that opportunity to break down how easy it is to become distracted. I have my audience think about goals they have set but that seemed to somehow dissipate without even realizing it. It can be too easy to simply forget the hope needed to keep stoking the fire of our dreams. Writing down goals, seeing them, reflecting on them, and checking our status, our focus, our energy, helps us accomplish those dreams.

You should not think that any of your goals are not big enough. After all, there is no shortage of paper to pin on the wall. If you want to purchase a home, buy a car, or land your dream job, try taking the time to sit down with a piece of paper and pen. That's all it takes. Give yourself the space and time to focus on your goals and start writing them down. Then, below them, list the little goals that will support the bigger ones. You'll feel activated as this simple but powerful act gives you agency over your life. This isn't about somebody else making it happen for you—this is you communicating with yourself, taking control, and giving yourself a set of rules to live by. Without rules, you can't define what a win is or discover the greater purpose for your life.

You'll find that you won't simply write one goal down, nail it up, and then forget the process—there's always another goal to achieve. Maybe you want to boost the confidence of a loved one or make a friend realize how much they mean to you. I've never found a goal that was too small to write down and check off. Just remember, no one can stop you from achieving your goals, whether you're in an unfair situation, have a bad boss, or have made a mistake. The only person that has the power to stop you is you. So, the ball is now in your hands to make the decision on writing your goals.

Recently, I found the goals that I had written down in high school. (Everybody saves their tattered goal list from high school, right?) I can still remember sitting at my desk and thinking so hard, impossibly hard considering what it was that I wrote down. But it was unmanageable for me to write it down until I had committed to the idea of giving my all to pursue the goal. That is the magic behind writing your goals down for yourself—they are for you and nobody else. And it's a lot harder to talk yourself out of your goals after you've thought long and hard about focusing on achieving something that seems out of reach.

My stakes started small, but at the time they felt monumental. As I crossed one goal after the next off my list, the stakes naturally rose with each passing year.

1. Play Varsity
2. Start Varsity
3. Be the starting running back
4. Be on the honor roll
5. Be All-District
6. Be All-State

There were times when I came home after a disappointing practice and saw the list on my wall and felt even worse. But it stayed up there like some unmovable monument. The pain of a failure is one thing, but the pain of giving up on yourself is so strong and everlasting that it's almost unbearable.

The list may have looked like it ended, but like all the lists that we can write to ourselves, a new one was pinned to the wall when a new chapter of my life began. By the time I got to college, a fresh list went up in my dorm room.

1. Play on ESPN
2. Be a starter
3. Score a touchdown
4. Be one of the top players in college football
5. Get good grades

The obstacles in college were much more difficult to overcome, the goals were that much harder to reach. But, having successfully completed a list in high school, I knew I could do it again. And I was right.

# STEP 2.

## SUPERPOWER YOUR FOCUS BY VISUALIZING YOUR GOALS

We have discussed the power of pen and paper in relation to your goals, but there is another way to supercharge your focus: through visualization. Not only did I have goals, but I also attached visualizations to each of them. Every string of words on my wall was set to trigger an image or particular situation that I had spent time imprinting into my mind. How do you achieve the goal of becoming a starter, getting time on the field when the ESPN cameras are filming? I would visualize specific cuts, fakes, and jukes. I saw myself accomplishing the goal in my mind's eye and, when an opportunity opened in front of me, I had a sense of déjà vu—like I had already watched myself succeed.

During my senior year in college, we were set to play against our heated rivals, the Iowa Hawkeyes. We knew this was going to be a competitive Saturday so, during the week, we had scripted out the first fifteen plays of the game. Our head coach, Dan McCarney, decided that a reverse would work great against Iowa because they were stacked with an aggressive defense.

Knowing that was the plan, I spent the week visualizing the way I should run this play. I would talk to my dad about what to do and get his input and run his scenarios through my head until they felt natural. The night before the big game, I laid in bed, relaxed and calm, imagining a reel of myself running the reverse play and scoring a touchdown. All I could hear was my dad's voice saying, "Trust your speed, JJ; make them catch you."

Game day arrived. Seventy thousand people were in attendance, and thousands more were watching the game broadcast live on ESPN. When I say my whole family was there, I really do mean my *entire* family: aunts, uncles, cousins, friends, mom and dad packed into my personal cheering section.

But on the field, I had learned how to shut it all out and just focus. The fans, the cameras, the music, all of it receded as I huddled with my teammates and heard our quarterback call the play. He locked eyes with me, paused and made sure I was ready. I was. I had watched it in my head before he even handed off the ball to me. I had been here before. Déjà vu.

We broke the huddle, and I lined up as a wide receiver to the right-hand side. Then, for a moment, I heard the crowd roaring, because it was ISU's first series of the game. I briefly took in the environment and then, just as quickly, shut it out. As soon as the ball was snapped, only silence existed.

I was already moving before even thinking about running. I saw nothing but grass in front of me, a pathway that I had imagined for myself was now turning into a reality. Things were different, of course, but the moment still felt familiar. The fifty-yard line was under and then behind me, the forty-yard line too. Then the thirty... I don't even remember seeing the twenty. But the ten-yard line made me think about where I was going as two defenders appeared on my peripheral radar. With a quick swivel of the head, I saw they were charging at me, cutting me off. But the talks with my dad, all the versions of the play that were already in my head and nervous system, all of my visual preparations helped me simply split between them and cut into the endzone.

I went to my knees. My teammates came running over and—in a sequence that was visualized—I was so in the moment that I could feel the connection and joy of what we had just accomplished. All I could do was look up to the heavens and thank God.

When I was signed by the Kansas City Chiefs, I saw firsthand how another person used visualization to maximum impact. During Saturday practices, the team would walk through Arrowhead Stadium before the game the next day. I noticed how one player would quietly wait for everyone to leave the field. I stayed behind to see what he was up to and watched as he silently strolled around the field. He slowly walked from one end zone to the other, obviously deep in thought.

He did this so regularly that I had to ask him what his purpose was for walking up and down the field. He laughed and replied, "I wrote down my goals for the game, and I was walking the field, visualizing various plays, how they would go down during the game."

This was familiar to me as an athlete, but for the first time I was witnessing someone else utilizing visualization at this level. I had done the same thing in college, but I thought it was my own personal method. I felt like I was a winner hanging out with another winner, birds of a feather in real life. It was an amazing moment for me, especially since this individual went on to have a stellar career. He made it to the Pro Bowl three times, was the NFL's leading rusher twice, was also the NFL's Offensive Player of the Year, and is now in the Kansas City Chiefs Hall of Fame—and I have no doubt that he saw all of that in his mind before he accomplished it.

When I was preparing to present the goal-setting lesson to the NFL rookie class I was working with, there was only one person I could bring back to help teach it, and that was my former Chiefs teammate, running back Priest Holmes! I made sure that the players could learn from someone who achieved great success by implementing visualization as a form of game day preparation. I know it encouraged all the rookie players to write down their goals and put them in a visible place. At the time, I did not know how many would grasp the lesson, maybe not believing in the power of a pen, piece of paper, and some purposeful visualization—but I recently read the Twitter post of a pro I worked with who said, "Time to write my goals down and get ready for the season."

I could tell that this player was deeply affected by the exercise when we did it the first time, and I was overjoyed to see that he carried it on in his life and career. He always had the potential, but I like to think that it was not only his ability to see himself achieving his goals but also writing them down that helped him become a starter and go on to achieve success in his football career.

# STEP 3.

# CARRY YOURSELF LIKE SOMEONE IS ALWAYS WATCHING

As I've grown up and watched the lightspeed changes in how we communicate and interact, I can't help but notice the intense pressure that is put on each of us to make an impression. Unfortunately, social media can encourage us to create a false image, one in which we're supposed to always act like we're in complete control of our lives.

Still, the one characteristic that it does get right is the importance of an impression. I cannot overstate the impact that a good or bad first impression has on a person and how it can follow them for their entire lives. Given the power of impressions, it's important to meditate on how you operate and what impressions your actions leave. Like a rock thrown in a still pond, the reverberations ripple out far and wide, often much wider than you imagine.

Impressions are complex by nature, so it's no surprise that most classes on "success" fail to address these fundamental components of human interactions. For example, in preparing yourself for a job interview, you might run through potential questions and answers, make sure your resume is impressive and you are well-groomed. You want to present yourself in a confident manner, but have you considered more than just your qualifications and the way you look?

Think about how you pick up information on your friends. You might have a considerate friend who smiles at people and holds a door open for strangers. A simple gesture like that might seem like nothing to somebody blind to the value of impressions—they can sometimes focus on qualifications and discard other aspects of what makes a person a good worker, a good friend, a good teammate.

I've worked with business leaders and coaches, and the ones that are special—the ones who know how to pull a team together so that the sum is greater than the parts—are those who notice small gestures and value them for how they can be used to build an impression. Technically, you can keep your job and live your life by doing the bare minimum at a high level, but it's the people who focus on the small things that make the biggest difference.

There is a successful chain of stores that is family-owned, and they had their own way of hiring team members. They went through the interview process and, without the interviewee knowing, counted how many times they smiled. Do smiles make you more qualified? No, but they do make you more likely to work well with others, create a harmonious environment, and make an impression on customers—they contribute to fostering a place where people want to work. How people gather data to form an impression is something to always be aware of.

There was this businessman, and when he interviewed candidates for assistant positions, he would take them to lunch. Unbeknownst to the candidate, he was using the meal to determine whether the employee would be a great fit for the company. When the food was brought to the table, he would note if the potential employee added salt to their meal without tasting first. If they did, he drew the conclusion that this person was not a good fit. He wanted to hire employees who didn't make assumptions, and this simple act revealed to him that a potential candidate would be a poor decision-maker and would not evaluate situations before acting.

Social media provide a platform for blunt impressions, replacing a résumé sitting on your desk. Nowadays, before meeting somebody new or looking at a potential hire, the first thing we tend to do is Google that person or check their social accounts. Keeping your personal social media profiles professional and appropriate is vital to being hired. Statistics say that 78 percent of employers use social networking sites to research current employees. Despite what some may think, most employers are looking for reasons to hire someone. The Harris Poll surveyed over one thousand employers and found that 67 percent of them look for information that supports a candidate's qualifications to get them through the door. This includes social media accounts.

Please try and make sure you are always aware of the impressions you are making—even though counting likes and hearts and views can be consuming, they are not directly correlated to impressions. In fact, bad behavior is often rewarded on social media sites. Good behavior, on the other hand, tends to go unnoticed.

A video went viral of a famous actor in a New York subway who was filmed without his knowledge giving up his seat to an older lady as the train became crowded. Talk about making an impression—we have a strong sense of what kind of person he is through what he did when he thought nobody was watching.

How many times has a public figure, with a carefully crafted persona, had their reputation tarnished because of something said when they thought the microphone was off and no one was listening? That reputation is like a balloon that can takes years to fill up but only one poke of a needle to pop.

In this era, so much of our life can be documented, it's as if we have a documentary crew filming our lives. The impact of one bad impression can be just as powerful and destructive to a life—whether you're famous around the world or on a school board.

One piece of advice my parents always preached was simple: "If you don't have anything nice to say, don't say anything at all." Being sarcastic might get a laugh, but it's much more impactful to be known as the positive person in your community. Keep negative or potentially hurtful thoughts to yourself, always. Give them time to marinate so that other perspectives can be considered. This tactic will allow you to focus on the whole picture instead of your own point of view. I can tell you from experience how much more effective it is when a coach calmly dissects a mistake I made. It feels like we're in it together, like we're on the same team—which we are—instead of on opposite sides of a ring, so to speak. In other words, be the person that people want to come to with a problem. Even the smallest extra efforts when not necessarily "mandated" by a coach, teacher, or boss, can go a long, long way in making your teammates not only trust you, but also strive to be better individuals themselves. One prime example of this is being punctual.

Getting to the NFL is a colossal accomplishment. So many goals must be met, so many skills must be refined, but the one thing that can diminish so much of that hard work is simply not being on time. Being on time conveys a consideration of others and a sense of responsibility. If a player was chronically late to team meetings or repeatedly did something thoughtless and inconsiderate to the team, there were repercussions and it changed relationships.

It is also worth remembering that always holding yourself accountable can lead to positive feedback from the most unexpected places. On August 17, 2002, I was on the roster with the Kansas City Chiefs playing a preseason game against the Houston Texans. On the stat sheet, I was nothing spectacular. In fact, my longest run for the game was only twenty-three yards. If you don't play football, then let me tell you that that is nothing amazing.

Since it was a preseason game, we all knew what was next—final cuts before the official team roster was finalized. I had given it all I had, but I sized up the situation when I was invited into the office. I was released shortly afterward and understood why—the team had decided to go with another player and who could blame them? He turned out to be one of the greatest returners in the league's history.

Of course, I was disappointed. My dream felt like it was over even though I continued to practice and keep myself in shape. I was prepared to try out again and made sure I was ready if given the opportunity. Seven months later the phone rang, and it was the Houston Texans. I was more than a little confused. Why were they calling me? How were they even aware of who I was?

Little did I know, they were watching everything I did during that August preseason game in Kansas City. They ignored the stat sheet and saw a certain character and approach they wanted. Sensing my bafflement, the front office explained how the scouting department kept an eye on me because of my details-oriented approach to the game. Literally, I had only been on the field for a few plays, but that was enough for the scouting team to make a recommendation to the general manager. I became the starting returner for the Houston Texans for two seasons.

Sadly, we all know that there are many examples of the power of impression working in the opposite direction. And just like the currents of a river, a bad impression is extremely difficult to swim against. I knew an amazing young high school athlete who was so impressive that he was being aggressively recruited by numerous Division I football colleges. He had it all: the football physique, quick reflexes, on-field intuitions, ridiculous speed, and, along with all that, he had the height too. His future was laid out before him. All he had to do was stay focused.

As scouts began taking more serious looks, however, certain warning signs began flashing. Very quickly, his reputation was working against his skill set. Some petty thefts and other off-the-field issues only made his situation more difficult. When the young man was on a college recruitment visit, he sat in the coach's office and talked about a wide range of subjects. The coach, aware of the player's issues, believed in second chances and wanted to get to know him before offering him a full-ride scholarship. Then a friend of the coach stopped by and introduced himself. The coach informed the player of his buddy's job: NFL scout.

The college coach introduced the young high-school player and listed some of his impressive stats. The player was surprised to have the opportunity to speak with an actual NFL scout. How many people get to meet somebody capable of making their dreams come true one-on-one, in a private office?

He thought of his friends and how they wouldn't believe what was happening to him. The scout laid down his personal NFL ink pen and writing pad on the coach's desk and began discussing the potential players he was there to assess at the college. Now he was seeing the inner workings of how scouts looked at talent, how they evaluated skills, little secrets that make impressions on people who create files and recommend players or advise teams to stay away.

Before he left, the scout shook the player's hand and wished him all the best. As the coach escorted the scout out of his office, the young man noticed that the scout left his official NFL pen on the desk. What was the significance of the official NFL pen? It was proof that he was in a conversation with a highly respected person.

Yes, a single pen may not mean much to someone in a world full of millions of pens, but it is never "just a pen." Should he chase the scout down the hall, give him the pen back, and then thank him again for the conversation or take the pen because the guy probably has a whole box of them at home?

He slipped the ink pen into his pocket.

Soon after, realizing what he forgot, the scout made his way back to the office but couldn't find his NFL pen on the desk. He looked all around and even asked the young man if he had seen it. Of course not, he replied. This was just a casual question, but scouts are scouts for a reason—they are in charge of making observations most people miss.

As he walked back out into the hallway, the scout told the college coach that this young man stole his NFL pen. The young man went back to his high school and showed off the ink pen. He bragged about his meeting with the coach and scout. Little did he know, word traveled back to the coach about the NFL scout's pen being in his possession. When the coach realized the scout's suspicions were confirmed, he decided against recruiting the young man and offering him a life-changing opportunity to play football at that college. A pen, an impression—and a dream was destroyed. I often wonder if this man ever realized the result that one small action had on his life.

I can't stress more that impressions have life-changing importance. By 2008, my pro football career was over, but I had developed a passion for preparing others to win in life. I also still enjoyed working in professional sports and had so many connections that I felt inspired to create a curriculum for NFL players to help them be successful on and off the football field.

Everybody in that world was aware of how surreal and disorientating life in the NFL can be. There is no way to practice taking that hit, that jarring shock. The intense physical demands, the grueling schedules; suddenly people are catering to your needs, you're flying around in custom jets, people are angling to be around you for insincere reasons. And then there is the exit, when the door slams shut. Few life experiences align with this blow, regardless of how much you think you prepared for it. We all need help, and sometimes we can get it from veterans in the locker room, a wise equipment manager, or a loving family member who ties you to reality and to what really matters.

But sometimes there isn't anyone there to help you along. My own personal journey gave me valuable insight and experience in the transition from life before pro football to life after it. This was such a crazy and frantic period for me that I wanted to help other athletes both make the most of the opportunity they had while in the league and plan for life beyond the game. I thought that some guidance from somebody who had been there could be invaluable.

I ran with this concept like I was doing the biggest school project of my life. I welded myself to the seat and wrote draft after draft of my proposal. After all, there wasn't any other program like the one I was trying to kickstart. I had to revise my methods and refine my lesson plan.

I worked to refine my program to the best of my ability and—when the moment was right, when the iron was hot—I submitted my proposal to the NFL.

Then, nothing.

Crickets.

Weeks turned into months. Months into years! The proposal went without a reply. Disappointment would be an appropriate word to describe my feelings, but I also had a faith in God and this felt like an idea that didn't even come from me—it was put there. Maybe I just needed to work on it more? So, I kept refining the plan, even though I had no official acceptance or job lined up to implement it.

I remained committed to my role in the community as a professional athlete, and my speaking engagements continued to increase in number as I incorporated my curriculum into my talks. I honed my craft, and when the occasion arose, I arrived early, stayed late, and committed myself to each opportunity I was given. As I remained committed to my work, I was given a once-in-a-lifetime opportunity to share my story of making it into the NFL as part of Oprah's LifeClass, entitled Dream Big. By staying consistent and dependable, I was building momentum in my career. And doors opened for me to speak to Fortune 500 companies like Exxon and Chevron. In my mind, these were the dashes and cuts and plays that I had obsessively run through my mind when nobody was watching. I was confident that they were going to be there, wired into my nervous system, when the opportunity arose. I had visualized it.

Ten years later, in 2018, my wife and I were invited to the Houston Sports Awards, which celebrated the most accomplished athletes, coaches, teams, contributors, and moments in the Houston sports community. It was a star-studded, red-carpet event in the city, with legendary

NBA, NFL, and MLB players all in attendance. I was visiting with a few of the NFL players I knew and ended up seeing the Texans head coach who introduced me to the new general manager.

When we exchanged greetings, the general manager told me that he remembered me as a returner for the team. That blew me away—he must have watched hundreds of players over the years. I congratulated him on his new role and offered my assistance if he would ever need anything. He thanked me and said that we should stay in touch.

Weeks passed and I was not even thinking about our conversation. I had offered my help to many people and, while it was something I was sincere about and prepared to do, I didn't expect anything out of it. On a Saturday morning I was about to take my daughters to the park, bending over and tying their shoes, when my phone rang. The new Texans general manager was calling me from the NFL Combine in Indianapolis.

"Hey JJ, I can't talk long but we have a job opening for the Director of Player Development role, and I wanted to see if you were interested."

I temporarily forgot how to tie shoes and stared out with a vacant look, unable to process what was being offered to me. When I tell you that I had spent many years visualizing a call that would have a great opportunity on the other side of it, I was telling the truth, but this occasion arrived like a diesel train.

After a decade, I had assumed that the train had passed and that my program was going to evolve into my speaking engagement platform. One week later, I was sitting across from the Texans general manager and laying out the program, now even more refined and fleshed out, as he interviewed me with the head coach. Within a few hours of that meeting, they offered me the job.

I often think of that NFL scout's pen slipped into a pocket as a parable. I know how it worked since I had objectivity and the information to see the whole picture, the mechanics of it all, but we don't always have that luxury of perspective in our own lives. It makes me wonder what actions like that built up my own reputation and gave strong impressions to the people who have welcomed me into leadership roles over the years. Not knowing makes me comfortable with the best solution possible—just treat every moment like it has the power to change your life. And in life's perpetual waiting rooms, I found that whatever I had to wait for was worth the wait. Not only did I get the job, but they offered me the exact same salary I had written down as a goal several years earlier.

People watch you not only for your talents and abilities; your character and integrity are in the spotlight too. The most unassuming moments can propel you into your wildest dreams or slam the door shut on those dreams forever. Are you prepared?

# STEP 4.

## IDENTIFY YOUR DISTRACTIONS BY WRITING THEM DOWN

One question I hear often during my speaking engagements is what it was like to catch an NFL punt. As a punt returner, you stand by yourself—about forty-five to fifty yards from the rest of the team—focused in isolation. If you drop the ball, there is no one to blame but yourself. The fans—always a part of the game—do everything they can to get in your head. The chants can sometimes feel warlike. It's in this moment that the focus settles, and all that energy becomes channeled into a single beam of intention. This invisible beam represents all the sacrifices, the visualizations, the goals on the wall, the millions of practice minutes alone and with the team.

Before the play starts, I shake my body loose and say, "Thank you, Jesus! Thank you, Jesus!" Then the ground starts shaking beneath me from the roar of the fans. Cameras are flashing, sports reporters are pacing up and down the sidelines, and the mascot is pumping up the crowd. The excitement makes you feel invincible, like you could run through a wall. No pressure, right?

Then, the universe slows down. After the ball springs off the punter's foot, there is time to study the arc, how it spirals or wobbles nearly one hundred feet in the air. Cheering fans and pacing reporters no longer exist, but there is the opposing team, in the periphery, running down full speed toward you with one unified goal: to try and stop you.

The whole idea of focus came easily to me. In high school, I would find myself doodling the word on my notebook, textbook covers, and stray pieces of papers. Before football games, I would write it on my tape. I made a necklace in one of my classes that read, well, take a wild guess. It got to the point that my friends called me Mr. Focus.

But you know what? I was 5'6". I had to find my inner giant to have any hope of making the pros. When the weekends rolled around, I'd stay home and go for long runs with a football in my arms. Even though I may have felt isolated at times, I was so thankful for the discipline God wired into me. By the end of my senior year, I was honored with First-Team All-Elite in Iowa, First-Team All-State, First-Team All-Conference, and a Division I full-ride scholarship to Iowa State University. I had stacked up some decent stats, but I do believe that my intentional focus was evident to coaches and scouts. And if it wasn't evident in my playing, then I'm sure they saw it on my tape—hey, it can't hurt to advertise!

The focus that really mattered to me, however, was the kind that kept God front and center in my life. That was the true gift of these accomplishments. The ability to focus on specifics brought the larger motivations of my life into view and, going into my senior year, I rededicated my life to Jesus Christ. I even added a new routine to my daily schedule: read the Bible.

Faith can be the ultimate focus puller. There were countless people in my life that had bright futures but became distracted. I've found that putting myself behind God not only keeps me humble and reminds me of what

I need to work on, but it strengthens my reserve—I can always call on or lean on Him at any time.

Having God in your life—firmly establishing Him as the ultimate target of your focus—provides a confidence that is unmatched. I like to call it a "Godly swagger" because it makes me feel almost invincible. This Godly swagger ensures nothing comes between me and my focus. I still must put in the necessary effort, but the rest I leave up to God. And regardless of how you want events to turn out, staying focused on God always comes with a reward at the end. Sometimes, you might think you're sacrificing a lot, but you have a promising future ahead of you, so go get it!

One time, I was dining out with friends at one of our favorite restaurants in town. We had placed an order and were excitedly catching up while waiting for our server to bring out the entrees. Then, seemingly out of nowhere, one of the other waiters dropped a glass dish in the kitchen and everyone in the restaurant stopped talking in perfect synchronicity and looked at the scene of the accident. My focus locked in and, after the commotion was over, I looked down and was surprised to see my food set in front of me.

I was shocked at the power of misdirection. I had been so distracted that I didn't realize that the one thing I was eagerly waiting for was right in front of me.

This example can be applied to your life—that promotion at work, finding your significant other, that opportunity you've been waiting for could be right in front of you but there is a distraction keeping you from being able to see it. In fact, 36 percent of employees liked their jobs less when they found themselves in a distracting workplace. Moreover, 66 percent of workers have never discussed solutions to address workplace distraction with their managers. When workplace distractions were reduced, whether through training or policies, 75 percent of employees were more productive, 75 percent had increased motivation, and 49 percent were happier, overall, at work.

These statistics were further supported by findings from a UC Irvine study that showed people compensate for interruptions by working faster, which, of course, comes at a price: more stress, higher frustration, unnecessary pressure, and exhaustion. In addition to the negative emotional impacts on employees, businesses also feel the consequences since even the briefest interruptions can double a worker's error rate.

According to Udemy's survey, nearly three out of four workers admit they feel distracted when they're on the job, with 16 percent admitting that they're almost always distracted. The problem is biggest for millennials and

Gen Zers, with 74 percent reporting feeling distracted. The opposite of focus is distraction, so I always suggest people identify their distractions. Ideally, you want to almost feel intuitively allergic to them. Whether you're running down a field with a pack of very large humans trying to tackle you or just trying to solve a math problem, it makes no difference—distractions throw needless obstacles in your path. Every time a phone notification beeps, it's an obstacle. A background television noise, obstacle.

Take ten minutes and pay attention. Then write down all the distractions inside and outside of your head during that short amount of time and you'll be blown away. This will also help you become sensitive to the distractions that we're rarely aware of but that might be holding us back from achieving our goals—or even harnessing the focus necessary to identify those goals in the first place.

When I teach leadership principles, I ask individuals to identify the top distractions that steal time from their productivity. Then, for each distraction, I have them write a plan to help them set boundaries and implement it. I always have enthusiastic individuals reporting back to me, amazed at how this little exercise not only increased productivity but also improved their sense of discipline and self-management.

# STEP 5.

# EMBRACE THE POWER OF POSITIVITY

In the 1980s there was a gymnast who captured the hearts of America and set the standard of being the best. She captivated audiences with her amazing twists, flips, and stellar landings. Her physical ability was obviously due to hard work, but it was how Mary Lou Retton approached life that allowed her to maximize her potential. She had a quote that drove this home to me: *"Rather than focus on the obstacles in your path, focus on the bridge over the obstacle. When you start seeing the bridges rather than the obstacles, everyone around you will start seeing the bridges too."*

I have witnessed how having a great attitude helps you accomplish professional goals. I've found that projecting a PMA (Positive Mental Attitude) emits an inclusive energy that makes others go out of their way to help you. It's obviously a very inviting personality trait. But having a great attitude doesn't just happen because everything is perfect. We must be proactive and intentionally choose to be positive. When you get sacked unexpectedly in life, when you find yourself on your back wondering how you got there, staying intentionally optimistic will be what helps you get back up. Sometimes it can seem impossibly hard to find a positive aspect and, when I find myself in that position, I always remember that everything in life changes and this will too.

Think of individuals who exemplify the power of employing Positive Mental Attitude—the list could include comedians, late-night talk show hosts, or even family members, friends, or coworkers. You find them laughing, smiling, finding the silver lining in problems, and resisting adversity. According to J.T. O'Donnell, CEO of Carreerealism.com, happiness has a magnetic effect that helps immensely when it comes to building relationships and increasing opportunities. Happy individuals are more likely to be recommended for jobs and introduced to influential people. Besides, people with happy personalities can just make you feel better about this journey we call life.

Same goes for the famous old-time commentator Dick Vitale. It wasn't just that he said their name, it was *how* he said it. I heard an NBA legend say that when Dick Vitale said a player's name it made them feel like a great player because he punched it up with *enthusiasm*.

Vitale had a way with encouraging words. Some of his better-known catch phrases were, "Diaper Dandies" (freshman basketball players who become instant stars) and "PTP" (Prime Time Player). He started his career as a teacher in elementary school and ended up as the head coach for the Detroit Pistons. Between those stops, he served as an assistant coach at Rutgers University and head coach of the University of Detroit.

Coach Vitale credits his success to having a positive attitude. When you boost other people with positivity, it not only creates a welcoming atmosphere but it also makes people want to perpetuate that feeling. People want to work with you, want to see you succeed because you are so blatantly obvious in wanting the best for them. How many careers have been derailed and structurally destroyed by the person's own toxicity in a professional environment? You just want to get as far away as possible from people who bring the bummer atmosphere, not to mention that, at an organizational level, negativity stifles new ideas and inhibits collaboration.

When I was implementing my Prepare to Win program for the NFL, I dove into studies that showed the effects of positivity, and I made sure to convey this to my players. In the most straightforward terms, I made it clear how powerful being positive was for everybody. You want to make the roster? Well, people in positive environments outperform others so why not add another skill to your already impressive skill set? Positive thoughts impact our heart, like the real anatomical heart, the one that keeps you upright and alive! Want to live a little longer? Want to get off the bench? Then take note of how positivity affects leadership in better decision-making. Help the coach make the decision to put you in the game!

I focused on positivity from the start because in the NFL—especially before the season starts and final team cuts have yet to be made—people in the locker room will be there one day and gone the next. I had a lot of practice trying to make sure I wasn't cut. But there was one time during the pre-season that really showed me the power of positive thinking. We had finished practice and I was taking off my gear and talking to a player who was in the same limbo circumstances as me—we were both riding the line between cut and not cut.

He was a gifted player with a tremendous amount of talent. I had seen him make plays that had the coaches taking notice, but there was also an inconsistency, something that seemed to affect his approach from day to day, even play to play.

It was obviously a stressful time and during our casual conversation, I noticed that every sentence that came out of his mouth would trend downward toward negativity. I was basically shaking myself up like a carbonated soda, generating as much effervescent energy and positive vibes as possible to make an impression during these last few days. But this other player was doing the opposite—it was as if he was making himself flat with his mindset that revealed his negative approach. He talked as if it was a done deal, and he knew the results. It became almost too much to handle when he said he was in a lose-lose situation.

This was a gifted player sitting in an NFL locker room with people who wanted him to succeed! I looked at him from the coach's point of view—he wanted to be surprised and blown away and impressed by a player's ability. Let's make him excited about putting us on the team!

But he was mired in negativity instead. I told him that even though the situation might not seem fair at this moment, try to remember that God was fair. I had faith that if I was released from this team, then God had a plan for my life. I firmly believed that something good was still in store for me and trusted whatever resulted. I just had to give it my all and then "let it go."

He gave me a sideways look and his forehead crinkled up into a confused expression. He couldn't understand what God had to do with it. I continued to give it my all, to make an impression that would make the coach keep me and . . . the following week we were both released from the team.

Unfortunately, this player never played for another NFL team again. On the other hand, my faith kept the flame burning and I continued training on my own and went on to become a starter for the Green Bay Packers, Houston Texans, and the Arizona Cardinals. I could easily have seen this player do the same thing—he had all the skills.

You never know exactly why you get cut—it might be a budget factor, or it might be that there is already another similarly positioned player on the roster. None of that means you are not worthy. It can simply be a case of ill-fitting circumstances, so it pays off to stay positive, stay ready to strike, and have faith.

We all go through life traversing a variety of terrain, experiencing mountaintop moments and rough descents. Regardless of gender, age, race, political affiliation—a life worth living is full of these moments. You will lose loved ones. You will create beautiful relationships. You will meet challenges and they will help build you into the person you become. What determines a good life is not what *happens* in it, but how you *react* to it. People mistakenly believe there are "big" moments and "small" moments, but I have learned that so many of my "big" moments are compilations of many small moments.

That doesn't mean you should never let yourself feel sadness or despair. Toxic positivity is a thing and refers to forced optimism, where individuals are encouraged to suppress and ignore their negative emotions, rather than dealing with and processing them in a healthy way. This can lead to feelings of guilt or shame; create a culture where individuals feel unsupported and unable to share their true feelings; and catalyze a lack of empathy and understanding among those who are struggling. It's important to remember that experiencing a range of emotions is normal and that it is not always possible or appropriate to put on a happy face. Rather, we should validate and acknowledge our feelings by approaching them without:

- Sarcasm
- Talking too much
- Criticism
- Judgement
- Lecturing
- Exaggeration

Instead, deal with negativity through active listening, asking questions, and trying to offer lessons through shared experiences.

My positive mindset and attitude are a central tenet of who I am. It would be easy to blame my parents and fantasize about how easy my life would have been if I was born 6'5" instead of 5'6", but I have been around enough tall people to know that height isn't a guarantee of success. In fact, I think my height helped me accelerate my positive thinking. I know a Positive Mental Attitude helped me in my career, relationships, and achieving my goals during challenging times. Whichever way you may be wired, know that it is always possible to change your perspective. It might take a lot of work, but once you learn that positive thoughts, emotions, and actions prepare you to win, you'll find the motivation to change.

For me, I find inspiration in seeing other positive-minded people succeed in life. Joel Osteen happens to be not only my pastor but also a friend and mentor. I began attending Lakewood in 2004, became a volunteer usher soon after, and have been serving there ever since. Over the years, I watched how Pastor Joel's positive messages of faith and hope in Jesus Christ inspired people around the world. He delivers his positive messages to approximately ten million viewers in the United States and several million more in over one hundred countries weekly. I can't tell you how many times I would go to church or turn the TV or radio on and hear a message from him that blew on the flame of faith and gave me exactly what I needed at the time.

Pastor Joel's messages taught me about making declarations over my life and the power of thinking the right thoughts even when life feels as if it is all going wrong. I love this quote from Pastor Joel's book *You Can, You Will*:

Every day we get to choose our attitudes. We can determine to be happy and look on the bright side—expecting good things and believing we will accomplish our dreams—or we can elect to be negative by focusing on our problems, dwelling on what didn't work out, and living worried and discouraged. These are the choices we all can make. Nobody can force you to have a certain attitude. Life will go so much better if you simply decide to be positive. When you wake up, choose to be happy. That is the fourth undeniable quality of a winner. Choose to be grateful for the day. Choose to look on the bright side. Choose to focus on the possibilities.

# STEP 6.

# MANIFEST YOUR PURPOSE THROUGH PERSONAL MOMENTUM

To a certain extent, athletes are masters in the art of momentum. We spend much of our time training, examining, and refining how to start and stop our bodies in space. In team sports, that art can be both seen and unseen. How many times have you witnessed an emotional turning moment in a game? When one team executes a series of plays flawlessly and the odds of who is going to win changes almost instantly. While that shifting of collective momentum is impossible to see, it is just as impossible to ignore. It registers like a temperature drop or a tidal surge.

Most NFL players have developed the wisdom to recognize what an explosive element momentum can be.

One play can turn the feeling of a sinking ship into a rallying cry for everybody to grab a bucket and not stop until the water is out and the team is sailing again. When this happens, you can feel an almost electrical charge in the air, and both coaches and teammates begin to move differently, talk with excitement, and start feeding off each other's explosive optimism.

The phenomenon is just as important and recognizable off the field, as well. A pivot play on the gridiron is the same as when a struggling start-up company brainstorms a wild new idea that transforms the fortunes of the entire year. Sure, a football game has a scoreboard, but companies have numbers of their own, e.g., the various charts to track expenses, sales, profits—or, in other words, wins and losses.

But, in your own life, when there is no clearly defined beginning and end to each competition or play, how can you understand momentum? The trick is that the win is in the process—if you work toward finding continuous momentum in your spiritual life, within relationships, or in your own mental health, then you will feel the thrill of victory as you manifest the purposeful movement.

Here are four ways to make sure your gains—whether personal, professional, or otherwise—are always compounding:

# FOCUS ON:
## STARTING YOUR MORNING OFF RIGHT

I always loved the saying "The way you start your day determines how well you live your day." Do you have a daily routine? It sounds cliché—and maybe even obvious—that a routine can change your life, but it is vital in creating daily momentum. A routine is a sure way to make sure you start your day in the best possible mindset. A well-thought-out routine is the ignition button on your daily mentality—on your winning mindset. It sets your expectations and gives you a structure to deal with, whatever the universe is going throw your way for the next twenty-four hours.

There is no single routine that works for everyone, and one Google search will show you there is no shortage of people offering solutions. So, I encourage you to look to others for inspiration. Still, there is a step that does seem be important for nearly all humans—and that is to make sure you're getting enough sleep. Studies show that adults need up to seven to nine hours of sleep to operate at their best while kids and teenagers can need up to ten.

We live in a time where people brag about burning the midnight oil as a routine rather than an exception. Sleep is often presented as something to overcome, not invest in. You know who understands the value of sleep? Professional athletes. Sleep is a major theme of training and there are curfews on the road. Decision-making on the field suffers when a player hasn't had enough sleep. Endurance is handicapped. Think about analyzing the millions of pieces of data a player has to process to perform at a high level. When I get tired, I stumble just trying to walk.

It took me some time to realize the power of sleep. As a kid I wanted to stay up until I passed out, but I remember my mom telling us that it's not smart to burn the candle at both ends. Study after study shows how taking well-placed breaks and getting proper rest improves productivity. Getting more done means gaining more momentum. And more momentum means more success. Sputtered movement isn't effective momentum. Lack of sleep messes with your weight, leads to physical illness and poor mental health. It also makes getting out of bed and sticking to a normal routine impossible.

Once you feel like you can get yourself to bed at a decent hour, the secret to cementing a solid routine is to start with a small, manageable process. For some, that means just waking up in the morning and drinking a glass of water. Seriously, even something that simple can have a profound effect on your day. Why? Because it is an act of taking control and proves that you have the ability to create order in your own life. Examine how quickly these tiny actions create a larger sense of momentum. Following through every single day will take a focused mind and deep sense of commitment, but both of those attributes are necessary to success, anyway.

Remember, sustained momentum never comes from a place of luck. It can always be traced back to hard work, dedication, and proper execution of day-to-day tasks.

# FOCUS ON:
## BEING CONSISTENT AND DEPENDABLE

One of the most difficult aspects of beginning a new routine is consistency. On my teams, I was never the fastest, most agile, or most explosive, but my small, consistent gains over time allowed me to eventually become one of the most athletic players on the field. Set a high standard for yourself and use consistency to reach those heights. I heard Denzel Washington say this: "Dreams without goals are just dreams and ultimately, they fuel disappointment. On the road to achieving your dreams you must apply discipline but more importantly, consistency because without commitment you will never start, but without consistency you will never finish."

Good habits are earned, and the consistency necessary to forge them will carry over into other areas of your life. Let's look at faith, as an example. I've noticed two things happen to people in their faith journey when hard times arrive: they either dig deeper and find a new level of support or they abandon it all together. Being consistent in faith is necessary to reap the full rewards of a relationship with God. That's because the consistency builds a sense of trust with God. When you establish trust, your faith can remain consistent regardless of your circumstances and be an anchor to get you through tough times.

Consistency and dependability go hand in hand. Can't have one without the other. Employees that are dependable set themselves up for longevity. One of the easiest ways to create an enduring relationship—whether it's with a coworker, boss, partner, or teammate—is to show them that you are someone they can trust. There is no set way to accomplish this other than being truthful—it's that easy. Sometimes, it feels so much easier to lean on an excuse, shift blame, or tell a secret to gain favor with another person. Be truthful to yourself as well as other people. If you say you're going to do something, do it. But finding ways to shirk responsibilities is a bad habit to get into. Practice on yourself and get into the consistent routine of being the same with others.

Unfortunately, we all know what it feels like to be on the receiving end of someone not honoring their word. Broken trust hurts as badly as any physical wound and can shake us to our very core. It can even alter the way we live our lives.

At any level of team sports there needs to be airtight trust with one another. I've seen firsthand what happens when that trust breaks down, and the results are often devastating. My freshman year in college was a big transition for me. Having to wake up at 5:00 a.m. for winter workouts in Iowa during the month of January was difficult, to say the least. I didn't realize it at the time but having practices at that hour showed the coaches what kind of players they were dealing with. The pain tested consistency and dependability, not to mention punctuality.

Numerous times I overslept and missed workouts. The first time might have been a mistake, but I really didn't have any excuse. Quite simply, at that point in my career, I didn't care enough about establishing trust and showing my teammates and coaches that I was dependable. As a result, I was consistent in one thing—showing them that I was *not* dependable. I knew I had the talent to play but proving myself as responsible was key to earning the trust necessary to get on the field. I also ended up having to work much harder in the long run to reverse the bad impression I originally made. So much momentum was going the wrong way, and the energy I wasted having to correct those early mistakes taught me a very important lesson. I had wanted to save energy by sleeping in and not running around in the freezing cold, but I did the exact opposite by destroying my dependability.

I thought hard about how to repair the damage I had done to myself and realized it just couldn't be done through words. I began to show up to practices early. I kept my eyes open and helped when I saw somebody needing assistance. I had to change the momentum—which is created with consistency and dependability.

It's such a "coach" quote, but I cannot forget this one because of my circumstances: "If you are early, you are on time. If you are on time, you are late."

# FOCUS ON:
## GETTING YOUR MIND RIGHT

*Your mind is a bit like a steering wheel. When you direct it with positive thoughts, your life will start to change because you are steering in the direction of your goals.*

We all know running laps can get you into physical shape, but what many of us refuse to acknowledge is that we need to take a similar approach to our minds. Make it a practice to think about positive outcomes. Do it over and over and over again. Mental laps are necessary for the times when circumstances get difficult. Practice positivity so when a negative thought enters your life, you're in shape—positive shape—to fend it off.

When I was signed by the Kansas City Chiefs, I remember a coach saying before every practice, "Get your mind right!" He wasn't being demeaning—he wasn't even directing us to what "right" meant—he was telling us to be purposeful about what mindset was going to bring out the most in us. Players loved it to the point that this became a de facto team chant. When we would walk by each other in meetings, one player would say it in the coach's barking tone. At lunch, somebody else would randomly yell it and get a rambunctious reaction from the crowd.

"Get your mind right!" turned into a slogan that bonded the team together.

# FOCUS ON:
## NOT HESITATING

Simply put, be aware of when the timing is right and then do not hesitate to take decisive action. The phrase "strike when the iron is hot" derives from a blacksmith striking a horseshoe when the heat of the metal is at the precise temperature to bend and mold what was unshaped iron into a functional form. If the blacksmith waits too long, then the metal cools and becomes more difficult to shape. I've seen so many people wait for everything to be perfect—perfect in their mind—until they take action. Most of the time, situations change without notice and can feel further from "perfect" than they were before. They sometimes never align as they did previously, and then all is wasted.

If I could give one piece of encouragement, it would be to always be ready to strike, which means always be as prepared as possible for when an opportunity arises. It's so easy to wait too long to act on important decisions, like starting your own business, going back to school, or pursuing a relationship. When the blacksmith is working, he must make sure he heats the iron to make it malleable so it can be hammered into shape. Of course, iron only stays hot enough to work with for a limited amount of time, so the blacksmith must strike while the iron is hot.

One thing you learn in professional football is how dramatically not being aware of opportunities, like a hole in the defense, can cost you. I spent years training, running, visualizing plays, and running patterns, studying the movement of certain players and team formations so that when the opportunity presented itself in real time, at exceptional speeds, I was ready to strike.

Translate this to your own life—take it off the field like I have. That is the beauty of participating in these steps. I'm not sure you can get your dream job if you don't strike while the iron is hot. Because, if you don't, somebody else will.

Even for elite athletes, your life will change, the temperature of the metal is always cooling down or heating up. I have witnessed numerous football players play their last down in college or the pros and then disappear. They might have been multi-million-dollar stars capable of incredible plays, but years later they resurface and try to get back into the scene. But the temperature, in a sense, has changed, with new management, new coaches, and new personnel who don't have an immediate relationship with the former star. Strike it all you want, but the metal has cooled and isn't malleable anymore.

If you keep your name clean, then you'll also learn the importance of relationships and how your reputation can keep a little heat on the metal. Leveraging important relationships in my career or personal life has helped me keep the iron in the fire, as they say, and also makes me retain focus on my goals and dreams regardless of what my situation might be.

What are some ways to recognize when the iron is hot in your life? Firstly, always be prepared—don't wait for the perfect time to start getting ready! Being prepared will help you identify when things are in your favor since you have been practicing them. When you have access to opportunities, you'll be ready to strike. Act by making that phone call, submitting the application, or taking whatever step is necessary to create some heat, and then pay attention for the right time to strike.

There are sayings that talk about being in "the flow" or "the zone" where you almost aren't even consciously thinking, and that is the result of hitting when the iron is hot—the exact right amount of heat meeting your striking abilities. And, in the passing of a second, a fraction of a second, things can and will change. Next year, next month, or next week might not look the same, so learn to recognize the temperature fluctuations in life and be ready to take action toward making a winning play.

# LEVEL II

## BUILDING A DEEPER FOUNDATION

W hen I was a kid, my family would drive to Chicago to visit relatives. Entering the downtown area, I always pressed my face against the window and craned my neck up to see all the way to the top of the skyscrapers. I had stacked enough blocks in my time to know that once you reached a critical point, the tower would topple over. And this was in my room, with no wind or other forces of nature. How on earth, I thought, did the skyscrapers stay upright and rigid? As I got older, of course, I learned that architects need to dig deep to build skyward. In fact, some of the world's tallest buildings have foundations that go nearly 300 feet into the earth. That translates to around ninety-three yards, almost the entirety of a football field. It seems counterintuitive, but the taller the building, the deeper the foundation must be.

We all want a life that takes us to great heights, so in a sense we also need to dig down and make sure we have a strong foundation. But what exactly does that mean for a person? I believe it requires constantly working on your faith, integrity, and discipline. We will all need different depths to feel sturdy so listen to and be honest with yourself. You will know when you're at a stable point. Be aware that your foundation needs to hold through stormy weather, flooding, or earthquakes. We all know weather changes and how important it is to be prepared for the worst. If we plan correctly, then we will have the confidence to handle whatever comes our way. Les Brown says, "You must be willing to do the things today others won't do, in order to have the things tomorrow others won't have."

We live in a world that often presents "love" as an emotional crowbar, used as leverage to get us what we want. If love is too comfortable, then there is the danger of entering an echo chamber. We must strive to be challenged by love; otherwise love does not help us become stronger individuals and partners. Likewise, having genuine care, compassion, and empathy for others—regardless of what you get back—is the second most powerful way to start digging that foundation. Gratitude is another fantastic tool. When you are grateful, then you can't only focus on yourself and, as you connect with others, appreciation and, again, love become a natural byproduct. Sharing is also vital. Share your time, energy, focus—whatever resources you can to help people. Respect is, perhaps, my favorite and the easiest to implement. Treat everyone like you want to be treated.

All these attributes and more are explored in this sequence and can be used to solidify your foundation. If you're sure it's deep enough and on sturdy ground, then you will be able to ascend to unimagined heights.

# STEP 7.

# BE PREPARED FOR THE OPPORTUNITIES GOD *WILL* SEND YOUR WAY

Opportunities are often camouflaged.

In 2000, I was a part of the Iowa State Football team. We had an amazing team and came off a historic season—the best ever for Iowa State with a record of nine and three. While this is not a bad position to be in before NFL draft day, the experts made it clear that my football playing days were likely over. After all, how many 5′6″, 175-pound athletes play in the NFL?

I remember hearing a person talk about faith, comparing it to being in a room and wishing for sunlight and fresh air. One way people utilize faith is by praying that God will fill the room with light and oxygen, and the other is to search the dark room for a window—one that God put there for someone to find and open.

My window was a call from my college quarterback, who asked if I could be his receiver for a workout with the Kansas City Chiefs. Of course, I said yes. How could anyone turn down such an important request? I was honored to even be asked.

The head coach, front office personnel, several other coaches, and the Chiefs' president attended the workout, hoping to get a glimpse of a promising future NFL quarterback. Again, I was just happy to be coming along for the ride. Just like my parents taught me, I introduced myself to everyone in the organization. I was polite. I smiled big. I basked in the moment.

Then, the workout began. In these tryouts, coaches will often start calling out plays. I worked well with the quarterback, and we could read each other—we both knew what we were capable of, so when he started firing passes, I went into full sprints. My heart was pounding, my eyes were focusing. I was locked on the ball the moment it came out of the quarterback's hand. I was using all the tools at my disposal. I wasn't *just* catching passes. I dove for catches. I left every ounce of energy I had on the field. After all, I wanted to make my quarterback look good.

Soon enough, the coaches began talking to me, and I could feel their attention shifting. Supportive cheers for my quarterback came next.

"Great catch, JJ!"

The stone faces I had been met with at the beginning of the workout had morphed into smiles and inquiries, as my skills began to draw notice. Worth remembering for your own next tryout moment is that people in gatekeeper positions want nothing more than to discover talent. They may have high standards and come across as unfriendly, but they are rooting for you, since your success is also their success.

In my case, what began as someone else's big break turned out to be the stage that God had been preparing for me. By the end of the practice, head coach Dick Vermeil strolled over, shook my hand, and said, "JJ, today you have made it into the NFL."

I walked in to serve a friend but walked out with my first NFL contract.

Here are two exercises you can use to make sure you're ready for the moment:

## FOCUS ON:
## SERVING OTHERS

I went into that tryout firmly locked into the mindset to serve. All I thought about was the ways I could help my quarterback shine. I found my way to an NFL contract through supporting my friend. It will never make you look bad when people see you supporting others. So much of my happiness comes from searching for ways to serve others. It doesn't matter if it's holding the door open for a stranger, making your significant other feel nurtured, supporting your family, or helping people at your job even if it's not technically your responsibility. In a strange paradox, the person who serves the most grows the fastest.

Here is a powerful word of advice: Never underestimate the power of serving others. Focusing on yourself over others has never made anybody happy—at least not over the long term. The self-absorbed may trick themselves into thinking they're successful and happy, but when you compare them to people who find joy in helping and supporting others? It's crystal clear who is winning at life.

Imagine having your hand closed. It would be tough to place anything inside of that closed fist. However, if you were to open your hand, it is ready to receive, and anything can be placed inside. Live with an open hand, an open life of serving others. It will not take long before you are surprised by what you get back.

Is there an organization, church, or school that you can volunteer at? I can honestly say playing in the NFL was a dream that came true but, I tell people all the time, my true joy and fulfillment has come by serving others and being planted in my church. Being involved in my church provided me with blessings that the NFL never could and led me to my incredible, supportive, and God-loving wife. Serving others brought out my gifts and has given me purpose and direction throughout my life. Is there something in your job that you could be a part of that would help your company become better? Do not think that helping others must be big and noticeable—the smallest contribution will often bring about disproportionate returns. Remember the power of a stolen NFL pen and think about how it might have changed that player's life if he had chased the scout down the hallway and shown the consideration and awareness to return his belonging? That small action, stemming from serving others, might have changed the man's life.

## FOCUS ON:
## STAYING READY

There are a million-and-one slogans, but one that I always connected with was "*Stay* ready, so you don't have to *get* ready." I was committed to staying in game shape, even when my chances of playing ever again seemed slim. I didn't just go for jogs every morning; I copied the drills and routines of pro teams in my neighborhood school-yard. It wasn't my agent giving me advanced warn-ing—it was my fear of missing even the most remote of opportunities.

No, I couldn't will myself to grow another foot in height, or be the height of my athletically gifted younger brother, Milan, who is 6'2", but I could make myself run faster and cut quicker. I had experts mock and laugh at my aspirations, but I continued to work on my craft and improve my skills so scouts would be hit with a powerful first impression: "If this guy was in such great shape on his own? Imagine what he might be capable of once we get him into our system with our support."

In 2012, I was called at the last minute to cover for a speaker that cancelled abruptly. There was obvious chaos around the event as they reached out to numerous people to find a new fit. I'm not sure who, but somebody mentioned my name, and I was thrilled to accept.

Upon arriving at the event, I walked around introducing myself to everyone present. There was visible relief, and I was genuinely excited to be there. Others took notice of my energy. I was smiling, easily connecting with everybody, and full of energy. Because I was ready to go before the call even came—and because I came in with the mindset to serve others—I was able to stay calm and deliver a speech that made one of the program directors promise to invite me back. That one, seemingly random opportunity led to a wonderful partnership with the largest in-school wellness program in the nation, which positively impacts kids across the country.

Still, I know how hard it can be to be prepared for a moment you aren't sure is coming. In fact, I've seen such scenarios play out all too often during my time in the NFL. A former teammate would get released. He'd fall into a slump and stop training. But he'd have the talent to get called up by another team for a tryout. A coach, with enthusiasm, would offer the player a fantastic opportunity, if he could just fly out within the next day for a workout. And then the dealbreaker would inevitably follow. The player would tell the coach he'd need a few weeks to get back into shape. Typically, the coach would say it's fine and that he'd be back in touch soon. Then the player would get into phenomenal shape and call the coach back again, again, and again, only to never get another opportunity. Eventually, the player would be watching ESPN as a headline scrolled past, announcing that that the team had signed a player in his position to a multimillion-dollar deal.

Never allow yourself to say, "It could have been me, if only I had . . ."

# STEP 8.

# CONSTRUCT YOUR DECISION-MAKING FRAMEWORK

Life, fundamentally, is a series of decisions. Studies show that on average a person makes up to thirty-five thousand decisions per day. I like to think of big decisions like a lion—king of the jungle. Tread carefully around them. But we all know the damage that small insects like ants can inflict—especially when there are tens of thousands of them. The smaller decisions may not seem life-changing, but they can have a bigger impact than you might think. So, learning how to make better decisions all the time will not only forge pathways to facilitate future decisions, but they build up your sense of self along the way.

My first job in the NFL was as a return specialist. Once that ball is kicked, a chain reaction of decisions must be made. The biggest, most complex decisions of the game? Not necessarily. But, as anybody who watches football knows, a game is comprised of millions of little efforts. Every player takes those micro decisions very seriously because we know the math—they all add up. The same is true off the field and in an office environment. Regardless of your job or career, decisions need to be made all the time—even not deciding is a decision.

Having a framework to guide you along the way will be nothing short of life changing. Here's how to get started:

## FOCUS ON:
## BEING CONFIDENT

Whether you are the head of your department, a politician, principal, sports scout, lawyer, or even a five-foot-six kick returner, decisions can be very costly. The first step in making good decisions is to find confidence in your abilities and skill set. How can you expect anyone else to believe in your decisions if you aren't firmly dedicated to your ability to accomplish the task? It sounds obvious, but you must first believe in yourself before you can be confident in your decision.

With the indecisive, I've noticed a tendency for them to rely too heavily on other peoples' opinions. They want to share the responsibility of their decision. They want someone else to make the decision for them. But decisions are microcosms of other social interactions, and it's great practice to embrace your own convictions. I've seen strong, inspirational people make hard decisions that nobody else wanted them to and witnessed how it paid off.

On the football field we had a funny saying: "If you are going to make a mistake, make it full speed." We all know that mistakes are bound to happen—one can look at football as a game of mistakes. But the point is to not be tentative—get behind it, commit, go all out.

Even if certain decisions lead to what can be construed as failures, don't shy away from examining those choices—no matter how painful it might be to study mistakes under a microscope. Being confident will give you the toughness necessary to become a better decision-maker over time.

## FOCUS ON:
## FOLLOWING PEACE

The second key is to follow peace and then decide. Indeed, do the work, pray, study, gather data, follow peace, and then let the decision be made from a place free from worry or fear. "Following peace," simply put, is trusting God with the outcome regardless of the risks or rewards.

On December 24, 2002, I had played exactly two pro NFL games when I received an early Christmas gift and was released by the Green Bay Packers. Let's just say that my locker had lumps of coal in it instead of a bonus. I dragged myself back to my hometown in Iowa fully aware that I, technically speaking, had failed: I was cut by a team and, officially, was no longer an NFL player.

I went into survival mode.

My parents thought I should go to Canada and play in the lesser-known Canadian Football League in the spring so that I could at least keep doing what I loved while having an income. Their advice was logical and well-intentioned, but, in my heart, I did not have peace about going to Canada. Out came the pen and paper, and a new goal was tacked to the wall for me to see multiple times a day. For two months straight, I worked out daily with the same routine I had done as a pro player. I was on my own with only me and my vision, but I imagined being in top shape when I'd get that call from the NFL. Even though my finances were constricting in an uncomfortable way, I made peace with my decision and committed to it.

Months later, my agent called. He said the Houston Texans were talking to him and interested in signing me to the team. I've already discussed this story, but this time I need to emphasize what the decision hinged on—my agent asked, "Are you ready?"

Was I *ready*? Because I followed peace in my heart and was prepared for my opportunity, I arrived in NFL shape and became the team's main punt and kick returner for two consecutive years. By trusting in God and listening to your heart, even when circumstances don't make sense, you will have an unshakeable faith that everything will work out for the best.

Will it always feel comfortable? No. Will you have doubts? Absolutely. But that is how following peace with faith in God and His ways empowers you.

# FOCUS ON:
## EVALUATING THE PROS AND CONS

This one might seem familiar, but it works.

When making a decision, grab a piece of paper, draw a line down the middle and write PROS and CONS on either side and then ask yourself: Will this decision benefit or harm me? Think about your core values and beliefs. Remember, a decision can impact your personal, professional, and spiritual worlds—so be sure to account for all three aspects when analyzing a situation.

Try to think ahead too. There have been so many times when I took an opportunity that was not the most financially rewarding but it was a great opportunity for me to refine my skills and give back. If it helps—and forgive me for getting a bit meta here—you can even think of your present and future selves as different people. Does a decision that will satisfy you now align with what will benefit the future version of yourself? Or will that future self look back with disappointment on how the present self handled a major decision?

The list needs to take others into account, as well. I have a good friend who is one of the most decorated college basketball *and* football players in history. During his senior year at Florida State on the court, he averaged 10.5 points, 4.9 assists and 3.9 rebounds and, on the gridiron, he completed 69.5 percent of passes for 3,032 yards and 27 touchdowns and rushed for 339 yards. Obviously, he had a hard decision to make when it came to which sport to go pro in. Everybody weighed in: coaches, friends, family, agents, managers. Because succeeding at the next level was going to take sacrifices from all those in his inner circle, he knew the choice was not only going to affect him, and so conversations needed to be had. As a result, Charlie Ward became the only Heisman Trophy winner to play in the NBA—where he contributed for an incredible twelve seasons. What helped Charlie Ward navigate such a big decision? He included others when working through the pros and cons of each path before him.

## FOCUS ON:
## EMBRACING MISTAKES

I always think of failure as a tool, and it takes time, imagination, and a certain skill to learn how to use it. Some people consider failure as an axe—use it wrong and a mortal injury can result, so they try to do anything to avoid swinging the axe around. For me, failure is like a screwdriver with multiple switchable heads in the shaft. I can use it to jimmy a door open, tighten up the loose things in life, take apart and put things back together after they're fixed. I've dealt with failing, so, fortunately, I have a lot of screw heads to fit so many of life's failures.

The biggest mistake with mistakes, however, is letting them define you. I've been inconsistent. At times, I lost my focus. I was cut from multiple NFL teams. I didn't start in college until my senior year. If I had scripted my life as a kid, I assure you, things would have played out very differently. So, at this point in my life, I could define my playing career in two different ways: 1) that I started in the NFL or 2) that I was ultimately cut and not re-signed by an NFL team. Which would you choose? The people who can fail, and not let it define them—those are the ones to learn from. They have retooled failure into a learning experience in ways that we all can embrace and replicate.

The inventor Thomas Edison is a perfect example. Apparently, it took him 2,774 attempts to engineer the bamboo filament that made light bulbs widely successful. 2,774 attempts! As the story goes, when asked about his long, lonely road to achieving his goal, Thomas said that he didn't fail, he just found 10,000 ways that won't work.

Cancel culture has it wrong—where would we all be if it truly means to have one strike and be out? With some very extreme exceptions, we all need a second or, in some cases, a third chance to make mistakes because that is how wisdom is captured for our future success.

# STEP 9.

# MASTER THE ART
# OF GRATITUDE

Gratitude is one of most powerful agents of wellness in our lives. Deploying it helps reduce stress, dissolve worry, and de-escalate anxiety. Bestselling author Melody Beattie put it perfectly when she said, "Gratitude unlocks the fullness of life, it turns what we have into enough, and more. It turns denial into acceptance, chaos to order, confusing to clarity. It can turn a meal into a feast, a house into a home, a stranger into a friend. Gratitude makes sense of our past, brings peace for today and creates a vision for tomorrow."

Unfortunately, we live in a society where entitlement often robs us of experiencing true gratitude. When I think of my accomplishments, showing gratitude is the one I am most proud of. I can tell you this—I experience joy for thanking the people who helped me get to certain points in my life, much more joy than from any personal reward of accomplishing those goals.

*Webster's Dictionary* defines gratitude as "the quality of being thankful; readiness to show appreciation for and to return kindness." The Harvard Medical School describes it as "a thankful appreciation for what an individual receives, whether tangible or intangible. With gratitude, people acknowledge the goodness in their lives and as a result, gratitude also helps people connect to something larger than themselves as individuals."

In America, we tend to define each other through our jobs. When we meet somebody, it feels almost instinctual to ask, "What do you do?" as if that answer will give us a complete picture of the person. It's gotten so warped that many Americans spend more time at work than with their families. The John Templeton Foundation collected data that outlined how Americans are less likely to feel or express gratitude at work than any place else. Oh man . . . that's a large percentage of your life to be dry of gratitude. Overall, participants were not thankful for their current jobs, ranking it the very last in a list of things they are grateful for. Yikes. We need to be aware of this momentum moving us in the wrong direction.

The article stated that 93 percent of those surveyed agree that grateful bosses are more likely to succeed. Another question found that 18 percent thought that gratitude made bosses weak, which is not only sad, but cannot make for a productive environment. Almost all of the people studied reported that hearing a simple "thank you" at work, the most basic form of gratitude we know, made them feel extra motivated.

According to psychologist Sara Algoe, gratitude serves to strengthen our relationships with others because it helps us identify people who are responsive to our needs and helps to bring us closer to them. Studies show that a lifestyle of gratitude results in being less materialistic, having more satisfaction with life, increased happiness and being in a positive mood. It also contributes to better sleep, less fatigue, better physical health, lower levels of cellular inflammation, and encourages the development of patience, humility, and wisdom.

When I wake up every morning, I approach the day with a sense of gratitude. My thoughts turn toward being grateful that I woke up with my wife and children by my side, and with a start like that, I'm excited to see what else the day has to offer. The ultimate receiver of my gratitude is God, and it always feels magnificent to pause throughout the day to express my gratitude toward God for all He has given and done for me. Taking a beat to acknowledge the position I am in to receive His gifts is a spiritual recharge that never fails.

I take gratitude seriously and make concerted efforts to cultivate gratitude within our home. My wife and I encourage our kids to be grateful. It's a simple process where we started to ask them what they are grateful for and they'd answer with family, their friends, for food on the table, and, naturally, their toys. Then it's time to take it to another level and have them think about why they are grateful, so they begin to understand there are a million things to be grateful for every second of every day—regardless of the circumstances of that given day.

Bottomless gratitude, and it's all there waiting for you. Pause right now. Make a short list of five things you're grateful for, and I guarantee you that you will feel better, even effervescent over what you have been blessed with. Seeing others, especially children, become excited about gratitude always starts a chain reaction—I get grateful for them being grateful! (Full disclosure—I may have put my thumb on the scale a bit with my children because they know when they say they're grateful for their daddy, it usually ends up with a trip to get ice cream.)

Here are three more strategies for getting better at gratitude:

# FOCUS ON: WRITING "THANK-YOU" CARDS

When I was in my role as Director of Player Development, I was tasked with bringing the Prepare to Win program to athletes to help them be professionals on and off the football field and to develop them into leaders. Ultimately, I wanted to make them better football players, but I realized that, to do so, they needed to become better people. So, I focused on the most powerful tool in my toolbox: gratitude.

I talked about players being selfless. That no one should feel entitled to be in the NFL, but, honestly, it's difficult to know how much mere words impact people. Anybody can nod and smile at the right time. I really need to make sure the players had a spirit of gratitude each day because this would make them better in practice, in the locker room, for each game, and off the field. They might be talented and skillful, but if they didn't possess gratitude and humility, they were limiting their opportunities.

At the beginning of this class, I put a pen and a piece of paper in front of each player and instructed them to make a list of individuals that helped them get to where they are today. Might be a teacher, counselor, parent, friend, or coach.

This was something to celebrate and *not* take for granted.

I wanted them to realize that, at the end of the day, they didn't make it to the NFL by themselves. Many players would light up as they recalled a parent, teacher, or coach. The conversations always grew animated, some brought tears of joy and overpowering gratitude.

I then instructed them to begin writing a note to that one individual. I will be honest—I have never seen a group of elite athletes dedicate themselves to pen and paper like I did with this exercise. They all took it seriously and would think about details that meant so much to them and specifics that changed how they thought of themselves.

Once the cards were written, I had them address and mail them out. Without fail and within days, the players would get mail back with beautifully expressed letters of gratitude over the gratitude expressed. Nobody expected this. We have become conditioned to watch out for people taking advantage of us, to be wary of strangers, to think a helpful hand is just somebody doing their job. So many of the players came up and told me how impactful it was to learn how powerful a simple act of saying "thank you" was to the people around them.

## FOCUS ON:
## GIVING YOUR TIME

How does it feel when you are with somebody impatient? Not great, obviously. That's why another quote that stuck with me is "The greatest gift you can give to someone is your time. Because when you give your time, you are giving a portion of your life that you will never get back."

Another part of my Prepare to Win mindset is teaching the importance and value of giving your time to others. A feeling of entitlement is one where you aren't giving anybody your time or energy—you just expect others to keep offering it to you. This, for obvious reasons, is not how you work together as a team. The best way to stave off entitlement is to give your time in an honest way. Connecting to others—being there to see what they need—is a gift that is not easily forgotten.

When implemented in the NFL, players began giving time to each other to talk and be available. Many of them had come from celebrated college careers but when you get to the NFL, the rate of rookies that don't even play or feel part of the team is higher than you'd think. Practicing gratitude and giving time to others created an incredible team atmosphere of support. When you express gratitude, success follows and here are a few examples.

- Our rookie wide receiver became the first rookie free agent to start in week one in franchise history.
- Our safety tied the second longest return for a touchdown by a rookie in league history.
- Our linebacker became the fifth rookie in franchise history to record a sack in his first career NFL game.
- Our tight end tied the franchise record for the second most touchdown receptions by a rookie in a season in franchise history.

# FOCUS ON:
# CREATING SAFE SPACES
# FOR THOSE AROUND YOU

I've walked into many board rooms and locker rooms. The one thing they all had in common is how different they were.

We've all walked into a room at a party, into a business, or even a home and immediately felt uncomfortable. It could be that you felt like you weren't acknowledged, or everyone was already preoccupied within their own circle. You might have felt like you were on an island all by yourself. In other environments, I've had people come up and introduce themselves, shake my hands, offer tips on local restaurants and to help me out in any way they can. I've also had cold shoulders, negative gossip, and divisive management. Thankfully, I knew that the power that created an uncomfortable environment can be pushed back against. You can always contribute to the emotional atmosphere around you. I would do it by acknowledging individuals and expressing myself in a way that makes them feel seen and welcomed.

Some employees never bothered to learn the names of the staff that they worked alongside or those they considered to have menial jobs, but I knew what a difference it makes when somebody looks you in the eyes, says "thank you" for doing your job, and shows you that you are considered equal, regardless of the number of commas on their paycheck. And I'll tell you this—you might draw a contract worth millions, but you can feel even less than the lowest-paid person on the team payroll if a coach, owner, or manager doesn't give you their time. Not one of us is immune to feeling brushed aside and alone in a hostile environment, so take any chance you can to make eye contact, learn a person's name, and really connect to them. Recognize that you are part of what makes a room feel welcoming or hostile.

I've seen organizations that believe in the philosophy of creating chaos in order to win. They feel that keeping staff or players scared, angry and/or nervous is the best motivator. In my experience, this just creates a toxic and unhealthy culture. It encourages abusive behavior, leaves emotional scars, and makes people do damaging things to deal with the stress. Sure, I have seen the approach reap short-term success, but never over the long term. Dusty Baker, manager of Major League Baseball's Houston Astros, once told me that in order to bring out the best, the fire has to be lit within someone and not underneath them.

Part of the program I developed for the professional athletes identified how lonely signing a professional contract can feel. Generally speaking, ask yourself who offers the most comfort when lonely? Families. I knew that any chance a player had to see and connect with their family was the best vaccine against the virus that is loneliness and depression. I had been through it before and knew what it meant for me to see my family and to have them feel welcomed into the facility. Having some of my all-star teammates introduce themselves and talk to them was a next-level experience for my family. When my teammates created a welcoming environment, the team always benefited.

I would always encourage players to invite their families to the facility and also help cultivate the welcoming environment. I made sure that I put an emphasis on hosting impromptu tours and, to show my gratitude for the trip, I would give a small gift to their friends and family. I'll never forget a note I received from one of the players' parents: "Thank you for all you do for my son. Encouraging him and pushing him the way you do. I thank God for placing you in his life."

As a recipient of gratitude, it made me want to refine and improve the program. If we know we've had a profound impact on someone's life, then we will feel the responsibility to keep helping others—and that is a beautiful thing.

# STEP 10.

# DETERMINE YOUR OWN SELF-WORTH

Self-worth is never dependent on a value that others give you. It's easy to fall into that type of thinking, but in a field where people make snap judgements, I've spent most of my life breaking down preconceived notions that have been pressed onto me. I know most people would think that a 5'6" man had very little value on a professional football field. But I knew my self-worth and, if you know yours, then it will only be a matter of time before others see the value that isn't apparent at first glance.

Talented people are used to others giving them value, and that can be problematic over the long term. Coaches pump them up. Trainers and teachers and scouts put them on the top shelf, and those accolades feel good. But when the player, student, or worker falters, they don't know how to build back their own self-worth from within. If you learn how to build confidence yourself, then you'll never have to worry about needing to get it from other people.

A lot of the most celebrated people I know never considered themselves the most naturally gifted, so they worked relentlessly to match their peers for whom it came easier. As a result, they knew how to create their own self-worth and weather the kinds of emotional ups and downs their more innately talented peers could never. They worked at improving their confidence as a daily ritual and created their own coping strategies for when circumstances were tough.

Throughout my life, it became easier to try to find my self-worth in sports, but I knew that I was going to be in trouble if I only valued myself as an athlete. Just like I challenged myself during drills, I challenged myself to always have a healthy self-image. This, however, was a game that demanded brutal honesty. I quickly learned that football is something I did and not who I was. When I was at my most celebrated, I made it a routine to imagine my life when the bright lights and cheering fans would not be there. I had to learn to be comfortable not getting attention while, at the same time, realizing that this was a special time that was not going to last. This awareness helped me find a greater sense of self-worth.

I'm sure this anecdote is slightly exaggerated, but I love the meaning of it. The story goes that a father is dying and gives a watch to his son. "This is the watch your grandfather gave me. It is more than two-hundred years old."

The father wanted to make sure the son understood value, so the gift came with instructions. "Before I give it to you, go to the watch shop on First Street and get it valued by that expert and see how much they'll offer you if you want to sell it."

The son did as he was told and came back to report the underwhelming news to his father. "The watchmaker offered to pay five dollars. He said it was old and has a lot of scratches."

Then the father said, "Go to the museum and show them the watch." The son was probably over it by now, running all over town with a cheap watch, but he went ahead and met with an expert in cultures and antiquities. The son ran back home and burst through the door in excitement. "They offered me a million dollars for this piece!"

Just because one "expert" gives you a value or a devaluation, never think that is the absolute truth of your self-worth. If you remain dedicated to your routine, make good impressions, serve others well, then, eventually, you will come across those who will appreciate your true value. Keep progressing and moving if you feel stuck in a place where your self-worth isn't appreciated. Here's how to ensure your dedication and drive directs you to people who recognize what you have to offer:

## FOCUS ON:
## KNOWING YOUR WORTH IN RELATIONSHIPS

Just like we need somebody to throw the ball to us in order to catch it and run, in life the right partner can make all the difference. A good quarterback is only as effective as his receiver and the receiver is only as effective as the quarterback. I like to think of life, in this sense, as the play, and I know the importance of having an amazing partner like my wife. There is trust that she'll always back me up, help me in areas that she is stronger in, and render aid if she sees me floundering. Of course, I persevere to do exactly the same for her.

It works because we both know our self-worth and recognize the worth of our loved one. Know your worth in relationships. Never settle into a relationship because you are lonely or just need to be with a partner at this point in your life. You want a partner that constantly increases your value, not devalues it. If you are in a relationship where the person does not value you in the same way you value them and yourself, then take some time to assess the situation. Think of the reasons that you are staying—is it good for both of you? Are you part of the problem by not asserting your self-worth?

# FOCUS ON:
# KEEPING TRACK OF YOUR ACCOMPLISHMENTS

Our lives are complex and full of various relationships. Your self-worth is constantly being evaluated and, in some situations, a different approach must be taken. For example, when it comes time to discuss a promotion or ask for a raise, we must have the ability to convey a clear, impactful assessment of our value. This can be uncomfortable. I have met many people who are only too happy to tell you about their greatness, but the real greats in my life are the ones with such strong inner drive and self-worth that they let their actions do the talking. They have a confidence and sense of themselves that is strong enough that they don't need constant reaffirmation.

Sometimes we will be forced to explain why we are valuable. It's easy to feel uncomfortable and stress over how the conversation will come across. We can either talk ourselves out of having the discussion at all, or we can find the courage to prepare and strike while the iron is hot. I've always found it helpful to keep records of your work, projects, milestones, wins, and accomplishments throughout the year. At work or on the field, it doesn't matter. I'd compile a quarterly or yearly report just to remind myself of what I accomplished.

Your track record will speak for itself, relieve some of the pressure, and help guide you in what to say. A lot of people and companies base your effectiveness on statistics and numbers, so gather as much data to help support your work and this will, in turn, showcase your skill set and the ways you have helped your company grow. When you finish and look down at your personal "report," you will probably be amazed at how effective it all looks together. And this all came from organizing your accomplishments and building your self-worth.

## FOCUS ON:
## REDEFINING YOUR SELF-WORTH

We live in a world that has weaponized self-worth.

Unfortunately, this tendency hasn't helped us improve and become healthier. Instead, it has turned many of us into fragile personalities dependent on constant illusionary affirmation. There are entire careers dedicated to designing apps, games, and social media in a way that target vulnerable audiences. Getting likes and followers can be just as gratifying a feeling as a gambling addict gets when sitting at a table. These tendencies can completely wreck your sense of self-worth, so really examine if you've unintentionally fallen into a trap that makes you feel like your sense of value is coming from a toxic place.

Do you feel like your self-worth comes from one or more of the following?

- The number of followers you have on social media
- Your salary

- The neighborhood you live in
- Your friends and their status
- Your brand of clothes, number on your iPhone, car you drive.

There is nothing wrong with working toward being able to afford the finer things in life. When it becomes tied to our worth and value, however, we lose our way. There is a saying that originally perplexed me, but, over the years, has come to make sense. A person seeking balance had the means to buy a luxury car and asked his mentor if it was okay to buy a Mercedes. The mentor nodded and said, "It's okay if you drive the Mercedes, but not if the Mercedes is driving you."

We know how empty having "things" can feel. You get excited about a new iPhone and love taking it out. The device generates pride as people comment on how cool it looks. You are up to date! You have the best and everybody knows it! But then another model comes out and, suddenly, you think about how much lower resolution the screen is, how "slow" it is, how the camera doesn't have as many features. What used to bring joy now brings disappointment. But the phone didn't change at all. The only difference is your sense of worth.

The NFL and other pro leagues are full of stories about individuals who achieved their goals and basked in massive successes, but, in the end, were left only with a vast landscape of pain, emptiness and loneliness. The saying "Money can buy a house, but not a home" is 100 percent solid truth. It's vital to stay focused on what you really want behind the object. "Money can buy you a bed, but not sleep. Money can buy a clock, but not time."

How we use our objects also shows a lot about our self-worth. In my rookie season I was signed as an undrafted free agent with a signing bonus of five-thousand dollars. I'm not one to be ungrateful about five grand—I was a college kid, had achieved a major goal of mine, was so thankful at that time and, honestly, felt super rich. I drove down to Kansas City singing along to music, banging to the beat on my hand-me-down Honda Accord steering wheel. Then I pulled into the parking lot and looked for an empty spot next to a couple of Ferraris, a Rolls-Royce, and some Lamborghinis.

Technically, I wasn't even driving my own car. My mom was still paying the bill on the 1996 green Honda Accord. So, I found a parking spot so far away that I knew everybody would have left by the time I walked to my vehicle. For the first time in my life, I felt so insecure that I even made sure nobody saw my car keys with the Honda logo. It was painful. Not because of how my teammates made me feel—they never would have thought anything of the car I drove. I was the one depreciating my own self-worth. I had to learn to untie my worth from what I had or didn't have and stop feeling so insecure. I had to accept and embrace my situation, and own it. I was living out a lifetime dream of playing in the NFL, and how I performed on the field had nothing to do with what vehicle I drove.

But you know what? Even if some of the other players drove cars worth more than my parents' house, a lot of them didn't let that define them. Players would sometimes ask for rides, and we'd talk about how great Hondas were and some of them talked about old favorite cars when they were in college or just getting their driver's license. I had made their success mean something it didn't and, when we'd talk about plays or laugh over old songs on my basic stereo, we celebrated our wins together.

If you're struggling with self-worth, keep a checklist and refer to it when your sense of your own value goes down. Remember:

- Your self-worth doesn't come from others.
- Your self-worth doesn't come from material things.
- Your self-worth doesn't come from your physical appearance.
- Your self-worth doesn't come from social media.
- Your self-worth doesn't come from your bank account.
- Your self-worth doesn't come from the important people you know.
- Your self-worth doesn't come from what others say about you.

# STEP 11.

# RECOGNIZE THAT FAILURES ARE OPPORTUNITIES TO PRACTICE RESILIENCE

Psychologists define resilience as the process of adapting in the face of adversity, trauma, tragedy, threats, or significant sources of stress. But resiliency is also a muscle—one that we need to exercise, so we can be ready to employ it when necessary. I know I've used it with family and relationship problems, when I've been injured, or my father passed away. And obviously, after being cut seven times from NFL teams, I've had some serious moments of workplace and financial stress. Essentially, I was doing resilience reps for four years straight when I played in the NFL.

For me, the word "resilient" has always had an elastic rebound feel to it. There was a saying I heard that stuck in my mind: "If you drop an orange, it will bruise; if you drop a glass, it will shatter; but if you bounce a ball, it will bounce back." I started calling it a "bounce-back attitude" when I needed to talk to myself and recover from one of life's "drops."

University of Alabama head coach Nick Saban once said:

> You know, people can't be overwhelmed by their circumstances. You get overwhelmed by constantly talking about negative things—how I feel, how tired I am, whatever it is. . . . When you talk about that stuff all the time, it just creates an epidemic of the "poor me's." The season is going to create tremendous challenges, challenges in every game. We've got lots of losable games we play. Lots of challenges out there whether we play at home or on the road. You've got to have resiliency to be able to overcome difficult circumstances.

If you were born with an easily identifiable "difficult circumstance" in your life, then being resilient might feel natural to you. My height was always considered a negative to most. People who knew my dad would come up to me and say, "If you were your dad's height, you would be awesome." People who say things like that never run out of shade to throw on you. Often people who are trying to speak down to you are the same people who didn't follow their own dreams. "JJ, you will never get noticed in Waterloo, Iowa! Look at how many talented players there are on real college teams—they're the ones who get all the attention."

To these people they were dropping oranges. Dropping glasses. They wanted to see a bruise or a break. Instead, I showed them a bounce with a smile. They didn't have to believe that I'd make the NFL, but they saw how I reacted and believed my resiliency.

In the end, my height worked out to my advantage. Since everyone was taller than me, I felt that they were the ones who were limited because they couldn't tackle me. There were plays that I exploited specifically thanks to my height. When defensive players wanted to tackle me, they sometimes had a hard time keeping track of me because I could literally hide behind an offensive lineman who was sometimes a foot taller.

In college, every time I made a big play, it garnered more attention and cheers because out of all the people on the field, the crowd didn't expect the shortest one to be jumping up to catch a pass. It is true that taller and bigger athletes have a better chance to play in the NFL, but when you take someone who doesn't fit the profile and they succeed, then you get both an unconventional athlete and a person who is a black belt in resiliency. That is a character trait that people pick up on and it never fails to make a solid first impression. You are declaring: "I have everything I need to accomplish my goal despite what others think." Celebrate your uniqueness and use it as a secret weapon to showcase how you can go further than expected.

To me, being thought of as the least likely to succeed does not forecast failure or loss. Instead, it simply indicates an opportunity to be become more resilient. The beautiful aspect of situations that seemingly set you up to fail is that they present you with chances to reveal what is inside of you.

A lot of people can talk and blow hot air about their fortitude. Since we can't see inside of each other, some people become their own hype men, constantly barking their own overblown marketing. But when everybody "knows" you are going to fail, and you find a way to succeed? That is the best advertising available for what kind of person you are.

There are currently 131 schools in the Division I football programs in the United States. Coming out of high school, I only had a scholarship offer to exactly one of them. I was not highly recruited, and Iowa State was the lone school to give me a full ride. My road to proving that I could play in the Big 12 Conference was a very long one.

At first, I did all I could to prove the naysayers correct. I showed the coaching staff what kind of person I was by consistently showing up late for the regular 6:00 a.m. winter workouts. I was making an impression and giving the coaches ample reasons to look at my height and assume that the assumption was right—I was too small to be a significant player.

Playing college football is partly about having talent on the field, but another part—that is often less obvious—is showing the coaches that they can trust you. Being on time to practice, honoring your commitment to school by attending classes and making the grades were all important to getting in games. The coaching staff's philosophy was, "Practice like you play." If I was late to the practice, then why wouldn't I have the same lackadaisical attitude during a game?

Due to my tardiness, which was entirely my fault, I created extra challenges in my first couple of years. So many, in fact, that I sometimes didn't make the traveling squad. At times, I was so off their radar that the coaches seemed to forget I was even on the team. I was constantly switched from position to position. I was placed as the fifth running back on the depth chart. Translation: there was no way I was going to see the field because only two to three running backs play each game. Finally, one of the coaches simply suggested that I think about packing up and moving back to Waterloo because I wasn't ready for college football.

One time, after not making the traveling squad, I remember watching the buses depart to the airport from my dorm room window. I was in tears, feeling sorry for myself. How did I get to this point? That weekend, I meditated on my approach and the kind of impression I had made on those around me. Clearly, there was nobody else to blame—this was all on me. At that point, I could either pack up and go home like a coach had suggested or do a 180. Truthfully, nobody cared if I made the travel team ever again, so what did I have to lose by at least giving it my all?

Almost overnight, I became a new person inside the Moses uniform. I started winning drills, being a leader, and showing up early. After many months of consistent effort on the field, I worked my way out of the doghouse and began to finally earn the respect of my peers and coaches. The coaching staff decided to give me one more opportunity, so they moved me to a wide receiver position during my junior year. I didn't just perform my duties well, I focused like a laser and exceeded expectations. I went on to not only become a starting wide receiver, kick returner and punt returner at Iowa State, but also team MVP, All Big 12 Wide Receiver, and Kick Returner. Also, I was the recipient of the Iowa State Impact Award— which recognized individuals whose accomplishments brought widespread recognition to the university and increased the involvement of ISU constituents.

I'm sure that part of the reason for my dramatic transformation was that I realized how close I had come to blowing it all. I was scared, not so much that I was going to fail, but that I was going to fail because I didn't give it my all. I had created my own adversity and had to overcome it. As result, my confidence sky-rocketed, not because of any awards I won, but because I knew how far I had come and how much hard work and commitment it took for me to get to this point.

I still had critics when I made it into the NFL. Players would tease me all the time about my height and ask if I shopped at Baby Gap or if I walked onto the field by mistake—the Pop Warner field is the next block over. I can laugh about it now, but I could have easily lost confidence because of the criticism. Instead, I looked inside myself and saw that I had overcome way more than taunting to get to this point. And I looked at the positive—I'm short and people get knocked down in the game of football. I had less distance to go before hitting the ground. The bigger they come, the harder they fall.

Nelson Mandela once said, "Do not judge me by my success. Judge me by how many times I fell down and got back up again." And we've all been knocked down many, many times in many, many different ways, and you can either look at it as repeated failure or practice at getting back up.

# STEP 12.

## REPLACE "I HOPE" WITH "I KNOW"

D oes it ever feel like others get lucky breaks in life, as if magical opportunities seem to appear in their lives but not your own? There is a cliché about luck favoring the well-prepared, and I've been around enough people known as "lucky" to confirm the platitude is true. Those moments that might appear to be mere chance—a beyond-the-arc three-pointer, a history-making field goal, an unexpected profitable quarter—are almost always the culmination of years of hard work. That sustained preparation leads to confidence, and confidence is often necessary to take the risky, seemingly low-percentage shot that, when executed successfully, might seem like "luck" to the unaware.

Confidence is a superpower. It unlocks the ability to charge into new and unknown areas of life without hesitation. I've used it in nearly every walk of existence—from the professional to the personal and beyond. Exuding confidence electrifies the space you move through. It opens doors and makes others see you as an asset and not a liability—a distinction that can be the difference between achieving your goals or falling flat.

Like anything worthwhile, however, confidence does not come without hard work and sacrifice. When I was a rookie with the Kansas City Chiefs, I had the honor of competing against one of the greatest punt/kick returners of all time. Coach Dick Vermeil liked both of us but knew he could only keep one for his fifty-three-man roster. On paper, we had similar stats, so the decision came down to performance.

During the 2001 preseason, we were playing the Washington Commanders (previously known as the Washington Redskins) in one of the final preseason contests. We both knew this was a monumental game in terms of our future with the team. To give us both a fair shot, I was selected to be the kick returner and my teammate was going to be the punt returner. We also knew it was more than just the coaches watching. In fact, our competition was so pressurized that both *The Kansas City Tribune* and *The New York Times* focused on our match-up almost as much as the actual game.

After we kicked off, their offense sputtered quickly, and the special team units went on the field to punt. There was a snap and then . . . boom! The ball sailed deep into the night before falling back to earth, where my teammate caught it as 50,000+ fans cheered wildly. After the blink of an eye, he broke free of the defenders and had nothing but open space in front of him. The crowd jumped to their feet with hushed excitement until he finally crossed the goal line, at which point the entire stadium exploded. His return was such an exciting and impressive feat of athleticism, you had no choice but to admire it. Besides, I had no interest in seeing him fail. If I was going to win the job, I wanted us both to be performing at our best.

Now, it was my turn. After the other team scored, I jogged out to the field and took my position near the end-zone. The whistle blew and then, again . . . boom! As I saw the ball descend from the night sky, I remember thinking it was my turn to make a big play. I told myself, *I hope I run this back for a touchdown, I hope I make a big play.*

Spoiler alert: I didn't score or make a big play. My "hope" was pounded into the turf when I was tackled after a short return. My hope was based on fear.

I didn't have the confidence at that point in my life to match my teammate's competitive mindset. Hope is dangerous without action and can dissolve even with proper preparation. At that point in my football career, I had the tools and dedication. What I was missing however was a strategy that put all my assets together in a way that made me *know* the only thing holding me back from an accomplishment was an opportunity.

There is a big difference between *knowing* and *hoping*. I took that experience as a major lesson and not only applied it to the remainder of my NFL experience, but also in every aspect of my life thereafter. I do not just hope things will work out anymore. I do the work necessary to build the confidence it takes to *know* an opportunity will work out.

This one tweak in our thought language has major implications. As you begin to recognize what level of preparation is required to be *convinced*, you'll perform at such a high level when given the chance that many doors will open. No goal will seem too formidable. Does confidence mean you always succeed? No way! But *knowing* you're going to win gives you a little extra gas in the tank and maximizes your focus.

Remember, losing is nothing to fear when you felt like you've given it your everything. Sure, the hurt will still manifest in your gut and mind. But then you just need to channel the pain into positive action. Losing can make you better, especially when you leverage confidence to squeeze all the potential out of your being. So, do the work to build the confidence. I promise, it'll be worth it, especially in this day and age.

Unquestionably, our society is experiencing a crisis of confidence. A Joon.com article by Amy Mezulis, PhD, published in June 2021 says: "A recent survey of over 450 high school students found that more than 7 in 10 reported struggling with self-confidence, and 8 in 10 reported that low self-confidence causes anxiety and interferes with school performance and social functioning. Self-confidence is at the core of many positive outcomes. Confident youth become happier and more successful adults. Self-confidence leads to better problem-solving and stronger ability to tolerate stress."

When I lead youth talks, I always offer methods to build confidence. During the most formidable years of growth and development, self-confidence is a keystone to a healthy self-image and outward performance.

On a personal level, it helps me to celebrate my wins and keep a record of victories, whatever they may be. This isn't an ego boost. It's a reminder of the hurdles I overcame, and a way to remember what I am capable of. The other option is to heap self-hate and angst on myself. How would that be productive?

When you feel like you've failed, deconstruct the situations and start to work on what you can do differently next time. Losing my spot on the Chiefs was one of the best things that ever happened to me. It made me better. I took what I learned from the loss and used it to form a new approach to how I practiced.

The more time you spend on yourself and your craft, the more you will be able to achieve.

# STEP 13.

# DON'T JUST ACCEPT CHANGE, EMBRACE IT

As an NFL player relocating to multiple cities to play for different teams, I had to adapt to a rhythm of constant change. Now, after almost two decades of working in professional football, I know only too well how changes happen suddenly, regardless of whether you are a player, coach, or front office staff.

By 2018, my pro career was twelve years over, but I landed a dream job as the Director of Player Development for the Houston Texans. I implemented my "Prepare to Win" program—which also formed the foundation of this book—to develop players into leaders on and off the field. As much as I loved playing and mentoring, helping people quickly became my purpose and true passion. But

I knew how professional sports operated. Teams could be celebrated one season and gutted the next. Coaches often came in with their own crews and, overnight, a seemingly secure job could become a ticket to the unemployment line. After a few years, I recognized a change happening to the Texans. It was like seeing a sunny sky transform into a hurricane. The team implemented leadership changes. When that happens, drastic shifts in front office culture are inevitable.

My wife and I prayed through it all and made positive declarations over our life which, ultimately, gave us peace. We knew that, no matter what, God was in control.

January 2020 was a new year and it started with exciting changes. My wife and I were moving into a new home and there was even more anticipation over the arrival of our third child. We began moving in on a Friday, the same day I received a call from one of the team executives, who asked me to come in to meet him and the head coach. The timing was unusual, and his voice was strained, but I went in and was immediately aware of a different vibe in the room. It was evident that the change had already happened, and it was about to hit me head on. There were no smiles, welcoming words, or even handshakes.

"Your services are no longer needed."

Stunned, I sat there trying process the words. "We are moving in a new direction."

I felt disorientated. It had happened so fast that I was still spinning when I walked out of the office. Disorientated, I was unable to get my bearings and felt like I had landed in the middle of the ocean with no life jacket.

I walked back to my car cutting through a thick fog of doomsday thoughts. "What am I going to do next?" "How am I going to provide for my family, one that is expanding very shortly?" "What will my next job be?"

I felt devastated because I had been with the organization as a player, ambassador, and player program director. Change happens. But why did it have to happen on the day that my family was moving into a new house?

I drove home dazed and told my wife the news. We were both astonished and spent the next few hours overtaxed, boxes all around us. And then the phone rang. It was the League offices, asking to speak to me.

"JJ! I have some news for you! Congratulations, you have just been recognized for having the number one Player Development program out of all the professional teams in our league!"

I sat back in a chair . . . or fell back is more like it. I laughed into the phone. But it was clearly a chuckle recognizing absurdity and not pure joy. What a day. "Well, I have some news for you," I said. "I was just fired from my role as director."

Now, I assume the NFL had some sort of poll with the results tallied over the past few months before they awarded me the win, but the timing was surreal, and it did weaken the sting of being let go. I thanked this manager who was now equally confused for how I got fired for running the best program in the league. New direction, right?

Again, I ultimately knew God was in control. This change was not so easily understood when we were in the midst of His plan. That's the thing about change—it's often unpredictable and doesn't make sense in the moment. To persevere, you need to maintain your faith.

One of the ways I mark my maturity over the years is by assessing how I dealt with change. Changes in my job, relationships, health, living conditions, and schedule. All of it, regardless of whether the change was expected or not. Learning that my success was not based on *what* changed but rather my ability to accept and embrace *how* the change would affect my life was instrumental in living life with more purpose and direction.

I discovered that to facilitate, adapt, and embrace change, you need to be aware of which aspects of your life are within your control. Then it is necessary to develop a strategy to deal with possible outcomes should something outside your control happen. Accepting that things are not the same might be your first intentional move. Doing so stops you from focusing on negativity and encourages a forward, constructive momentum.

In November 2016, shortly after Thanksgiving, I dealt with one of my most difficult, life-altering changes. While sleeping and only two days after his sixty-fifth birthday, my father passed away. I was left without my best friend, mentor, and the person I talked to multiple times a day. There were dreams I wished to accomplish with him by my side. I grieved the grandfather my children loved and the moments of their life he would not be a part of, like the birth of my son. I grieved my parents' togetherness, how they were always side by side, and now my mom having to navigate life without her other half.

As difficult as the loss was, and will always be, I embraced the pain and sadness to celebrate not only the life he led but also the hero he was to so many, including myself. I was able to move forward knowing that I gave everything I had to build a strong relationship with my father. There was nothing left unspoken or unshared between us—he knew how I felt about him, and I knew how my father felt about me. When I struggle with a new change, instead of being able to pick up the phone and hear his voice in my ear, I hear it inside of me as he says, "Dig deep, Baby!"

Before the pandemic, life consisted of lifestyle activities like going out to eat, hitting the gym, celebrating special moments with your family and friends, concerts, sporting events, working in an office space—you know, stuff we all considered normal. However, the world *changed*. Overnight, even going to the grocery store seemed like an adventure, like every bag of potatoes was coated with the deadly virus. Social distancing became a new norm, just like mask wearing, zoom meetings, and remote working.

At the same time, I had just moved into my new home and been fired from my job. It was easy to become fearful and discouraged but I had to remain positive despite not knowing what the next step would be. My wife and I had a supernatural peace that I can't fully explain except to say, faith. We knew God was in control. I knew to win, I had to direct my emotions in a positive way, focus on a healthy self-image, and remain optimistic. It's in these pivotal moments that you begin to uncover your true destiny.

Little did I know that, despite such life-changing events, my family and I were about to enter one of the most precious seasons together as a new family of five. I won't trade the moments we shared in 2020 for anything in the world because despite the horrible disaster around us—we were in a sweet spot. That major change allowed me to finish writing the book you are reading, a project I started many years ago. And, in the midst of the pandemic, a few short months after losing my job, the NFL office called and asked if I would be interested in a new role working with all former players that reside in the state of Texas. I assume that the job I was fired from made an impression on the organization that gave me an award for it. Just like when that preseason loss got me cut from the roster but also got me noticed, and ultimately hired, by the opposing team.

Embracing change can be instrumental to putting you on the road for greater things ahead. Let change force innovation inside of you.

# STEP 14.

# LETTING GO AND FINDING YOUR OWN STRIDE

I f you live your life focusing on who wronged you, the ones that hated on you, the supposed friends who left you behind, you will end up dragging a lot of useless weight into the future. All of that is a bag of bricks and you have to it go.

Letting go can sometimes sound easy, but it takes a lot of perspective-changing and forgiveness to release that angry grip. What makes it worth the effort is, regardless of circumstances, putting an end to the emotional damage the anger causes. If we're hurt and bitter and can't get past an experience, we're only doing damage to ourselves.

The old saying "Hate destroys the vessel it's kept in" carries some hard truth.

Growing up, I would hear stories about my dad's football career. He was impressive, and his accomplishments were on a steady repeat. "Did you know your dad scored thirty-seven touchdowns?" "Hey, JJ, are you going to be like your dad, an All-American and the best running back in the state?" "Your dad had a stack so high of college scholarships that he had to pile them in the corner of his room. Seriously, he had over one hundred offers."

As a kid, I was so curious and fascinated with all of these stories because my dad never brought up his accolades, trophies, or records. He never sat around and pulled out the old scrapbook and gathered us around to hear the Legend of Dad stories. But he was my father! I looked up to him like most young kids do. I always asked him questions because I wanted to follow in his footsteps. And every time I would bring a story up, he would give me the same response. In a monotone, slow voice that carried fatherly force, he would say, "JJ, let it go." Whenever his friends would come over and start reminiscing about high school sports and he was brought up, he would say, "Hey, let it go!" He never said it in an angry tone, and it wasn't false humility. The delivery was something I didn't understand until I was an adult. Dad did not dwell on the past because he was in the moment and that is where he found the most peace and happiness. He did not want to reside in some faded glory days and miss what was in front of him.

This was one of the greatest lessons he ever gave me in my life. Without saying as much, he laid out what to prioritize and what to let go. He wasn't saying "let it go" regarding his accomplishments—I do think he was proud of them—but he didn't want to let them be the only thing that defined him.

From time to time, I will get caught up in something, maybe become emotional when it's not called for, and I'll take a breath and hear my dad say, "Let it go"—and often, he'd have this laugh that put it in context. There was no bitterness, as if they were painful moments that still stung and he didn't want them brought up—it was a reminder to focus on right now.

There were so many times in my life that those three words allowed me to release the grip on disappointments. By keeping your focus on God, it makes it a lot easier to let go of the petty stuff in our lives that can steal our focus and attention.

- I had to let go that I was released and let go as a player in the NFL seven times.

- I had to let go of the individuals who were critical of me.
- I had to let go of the people who had treated me wrong.
- I had to let go of things that were holding me back.
- I had to let go of things that did not make sense.
- I had to let go of things that did not work out.
- I had to let go that I was fired from my job.
- I had to let go of not being in control.
- I had to let go of worry.
- I had to let go of grief.
- I had to let go of doubt.
- I had to let go of fear.
- I had to let go . . .

Letting go is a fundamental step in preparing you to win. Sometimes I hear people talk about defeats, mistakes, and experiences from over thirty years ago. Their focus is so strong that you'd almost think it just happened to them! It takes so much work to keep something negative like that alive and burning in your life. Imagine if you can repurpose that energy into a positive and help create momentum. Not being able to let go is like tying an anchor to your forward momentum—it can simply deplete you if you're not careful.

Here is the best way to keep moving forward, regardless of the obstacles in your way:

# FOCUS ON:
# FINDING YOUR STRIDE

Do you ever feel like you're inside an echo chamber where voices of experts are bouncing off the walls, touting their credentials, yelling at us that *now* is the time to buy the home, *now* is the time to buy this stock, and that this expensive school is the only one to send your kids to? I certainly do.

Whether it comes from economists, family, or friends, this type of "advice" can sow discouragement. It has the tendency to make you feel lacking and inflames fear of missing out. And in our current social state where we are bombarded with social media notifications, this fear of missing out can become inescapable. "Look who just bought the new ____!" "Look where ____ is vacationing!" "____ is at a party and I'm at home alone in my sweatpants." All considering, how can you not feel like everyone is flourishing except you?

While constant effort is needed to manage the feelings of fear of missing out, try to think of your progress through life as a marathon—just keep moving forward at a pace that is comfortable for you to keep jogging at. Some people sprint at the beginning and burn out by the end, but if you can tune in to your own natural pace, then you can stay steady and make it to the finish line in your own time.

After all, wouldn't you rather wait for your dreams than try to live in someone else's? Dreams are not one size fits all. Trust a guy who saw some of the best athletes in the world running at him and away from him—*everybody* has a unique stride. The ones who excel are the ones who don't try to copy somebody else—they know what works for them. People move at different times and in different ways. Some stutter step, some blast off the blocks, and some start in a low gear and turn into diesel trains by the end.

There will come a time when you celebrate a friend's promotion while waiting on your own. The time will come when everyone around you is getting married and having children and you are still waiting to meet the right partner. The time will come when you're standing on the sidelines watching everyone else run.

"Don't compare your life to others. There's no comparison between the sun and the moon, they shine when it's their time." These words are from India's ex-president, A. P. J. Abdul Kalam, and they are words to live by.

When you are in your true stride, you know it because you aren't concerned by what anybody else is posting, what they just purchased, or what you are missing out on. Your focus will be straight ahead, on the journey toward your dreams and the peace that it brings you.

Finding your stride does not mean you take every opportunity that comes your way. Be genuine to yourself, your passions, beliefs, and skill set. I remember my freshman and sophomore years in college, when I was trying to earn playing time as a running back. With my height and weight, I thought it would be a great idea to bulk up and to play more physical. I hit the gym, stuck in my ear buds, and pumped iron, imagining myself bulking up. I was going to be like a terrifying cannonball shooting across the field!

But my height and less bulky frame were contributing factors to my gift because they allowed me to be swift and dart around like nobody else on the field. Luckily, I learned quickly that my "genius" plan to pack on weight was going to take me off my natural stride and make me less effective.

In your case, you might think you need to be more outgoing when you are wired to be chill and laid back, or you have a natural talent for working behind the scenes but feel like you need to be out front garnering immediate validation. Again, it's different for everybody and that's why it's easy to place trust in your stride. When you do, the result might not be what others imagined, but there will be a natural contentment that is unmistakable.

I'm getting older, and if I know one thing, it's that bodies change as they age. Strides change as life does, so you must constantly ensure that your stride remains yours. My stride was different when I was playing pro football, but it was true to myself, just as my adjusted stride is right for me in this moment, wherever I might be.

# LEVEL III

## FORGE AN UNSTOPPABLE TEAM CULTURE

During college, I would often find myself looking toward the night sky. In Iowa, the stars seemed like they had their high beams on—and I loved thinking about how energy is so powerful that you can literally see it from the other end of the universe.

I have seen humans who operate in the same way. It's simple to run drills, follow instructions and whistles, check boxes that others put in front of you. But that is mostly physical exertion and, since we are all built with different bodies, excelling at motor skill activities often leans more on anatomy than anything else. I've found that there is a major component to winning that is often overlooked: our inner strength.

When I trained, I took it upon myself to not only work on my physical abilities, but I also made sure that I was developing my inner qualities. We've all heard the stories of talented individuals who, ultimately, never lived up to their potential. Think of your childhood and how one or two kids were naturally the smartest, fastest, most popular, or most athletic. Kids like this seemed to have a head start on the rest of us, right?

But why didn't they all make an Olympic team or make it in Hollywood?

Because excelling at elite levels demands so much more than physical prowess and innate talent. I've seen too many gifted individuals derailed by peer pressure, adversity, and other personal setbacks that inevitably come their way. We live in a society filled with distractions that can easily drain our energy. The most *successful* people I know have had one thing in common—they realized the power of being surrounded by a winning culture. As a result, they never thought they were the best. They always found ways to improve, realizing that, to stay on top, they needed to be pushed by a group of peers. And if that culture didn't exist? They used their leadership skills to build one from scratch.

Society might encourage you to worry about what people think of you, but when you are firm in your beliefs and principles, then your core values inevitably become part of the culture you surround yourself with. If a person is defined by their principles, then so is a group. For example, if you hang out with people who deepen their relationship with God—such as taking time to pray, meditate, read scriptures, and practice living with a grateful heart—then you will too.

Social balance is necessary to channel your inner energy into action, so make sure to check in with yourself and those around you on a daily basis. If you do, no problem will seem too complicated to overcome. You can't do it alone. Treat obstacles as opportunities to strengthen your connection with those around you.

A supportive group can help you stay stable. And mental stability leads to success. Once you recognize the power of a team, you'll never want to be without one—whether off or on the field. From novel communication techniques to proven leadership practices, Level III takes all the lessons you've learned throughout the rest of the book and applies them outwardly, so you can find, form, or grow an unstoppable team culture.

# STEP 15.

## SURROUND YOURSELF WITH WINNERS

First, let's examine what a "winner" is, since that label and its opposite are thrown around in all kinds of reckless ways. Whether you are in school or in the office, the traits of a "winner" are undeniable. They are motived individuals who never seem to settle for where they are. There is a curiosity and drive to keep pushing themselves to find a greater purpose for their lives that reflects their mission and values. Winners are not about dominating "losers." In fact, winners should have the reverse effect and be making everyone around them better.

Being famous does not automatically make you a winner. Neither does extreme wealth or popularity—that is what a manipulated society, unfortunately, deems as some sort of winning. Ultimately, it's not about what society says is winning. It's about what you know to be true when you work on yourself. I can see a kid on the playground and watch how he interacts with others, how he pushes himself and shows compassion for a hurt friend or protects somebody from a cross word or bullying, and I'm inspired by that winner. Age, income, or how many followers you have do not factor into winning. Individuals who have a purpose inspire others and, as the saying goes, birds of a feather flock together. So, if you hang out with people who lie, chances are you will start to be influenced by how lies are used by people. If you hang with people who abuse drugs, chances are that their choices will influence you and drag you down until eventually you're joining in.

My wins in life start with winning at home, but your wins might be encouraged by a friend or a mentor or even a pastor delivering an inspiring sermon. Winners inspire others without even trying. My family is everything to me, and I was taught of that importance from an early age by my parents. It's not your career, your title, your bank account, or your influence that matters most to winners—it's the people they call family.

That is a winner's point of view.

The foundation of the family is so important in creating winners. Statistics say that when a father is not actively involved in his child's life, the child will be twice as likely to drop out of school, 54 percent more likely to make less money than their parents, seven times more likely to experience teen pregnancy, and the incarceration rate increases as well. The effects of not having a mother also creates hurdles that are difficult to overcome. There can be low self-esteem, depression, anxiety, lack of motivation, and developmental problems. These factors can have a devastating impact on a child's social and emotional development.

And part of being a winner is constantly challenging yourself and the role you play in your groups. I regularly take time to reflect and ask myself "Am I being a good husband, father, son, brother, uncle, or friend?" If I answer no, then I need to prioritize those aspects of my life. Being a winner doesn't mean always being right—it means always truthfully looking at your actions and trying to improve. A winner isn't awarded the title and then gets to drop all the effort that went into it.

To surround yourself with winners, however, it's important to come across as one. First impressions set the tone for future interactions and can greatly influence how others perceive and interact with us. They can even determine whether a potential friendship will develop. For example, a confident and friendly demeanor can make others more likely to approach us and be open to building a friendship. On the other hand, if we appear unapproachable or unfriendly, it may discourage others from interacting with us.

First impressions are made in the first thirty seconds of meeting someone.

Let me repeat that: a person forms an opinion of you in less time than it takes to drink a glass a water. Statistics say 55 percent of first impressions are made by what we see (visual), 38 percent the way we hear your first words (vocal), and 7 percent the actual words you say (verbal). According to *Forbes*, our brains make a thousand computations in the initial seven seconds we see someone. Are you trustworthy, confident, likeable, or competent? Within seconds a decision has been made, even though you probably haven't even said, "Hello."

For example, my wife and I were in the process of looking for a realtor a few years ago. One day, we made a phone call to a potential agent, and we took immediate notice of her tone of voice, energy, and how she communicated information to us. Considering it was a first impression, the immediate feeling we had was that she lacked positivity that was impossible to surmount, no matter how much she impressed us in other areas. So, guess what happened? My wife and I decided to work with someone else. We ended up meeting realtors who were not only positive, kind, and friendly, but also incredibly professional. With their help, we found our home and now they are like family to us.

The first impression made all the difference. It always does.

There are three keys that I believe are important in making a solid first impression. I like to call it the KLP Factor—Knowledge, Likeability, and Passion.

## FOCUS ON: KNOWLEDGE

You have probably heard the phrase "knowledge is power." If you are in sales, know your product. If you're a pilot, know your plane. If you're a quarterback, know your plays. If you're a waiter, know your menu. When you have the knowledge, you can't help but be confident. And when you're confident, you win.

Knowledge is the framework for performance. No matter how in shape you are, how well dressed, what kind of car you drive; none of it is going to help you progress without knowledge. Those who are willing to spend the time necessary to hit the books and learn more than the bare minimum will be the ones who succeed. On some level, it really is *that* simple—even in the NFL.

So, if you are an intern looking to land a full-time job at the company, learn as much as possible about what the company does, who works there, and why they are doing well or struggling. While this kind of work might not be a prerequisite for applying or even getting hired, it will certainly be the reason that internship turns into a job. Be willing to put in the additional work. Go the extra mile. Dedicate yourself to learning all that you can so you can be prepared to win when your number is called.

Take the example of Kurt Warner. Here was a backup quarterback that not only led his team to the Super Bowl, but he won it with MVP honors. How did he go from third string to Super Bowl MVP? When his opportunity came, he came armed with knowledge necessary to perform at an elite level. That means there were countless games that he studied, practiced, and prepared for, without any payoff. We're talking thousands of hours of reviewing game tape, meetings, and playbook reviews. All of it, seemingly, for naught. Or at least that's what a lesser competitor would think.

If you want to know what it takes to be one of the best football players of all time, then look at Kurt Warner before he ever started in the NFL. Instead of time on the bench, he considered it time to gain the knowledge necessary to succeed when his number was finally called. When I was with the Arizona Cardinals, I had the opportunity to be teammates with Kurt. In the meeting rooms, while some were on the brink of nodding off, he was alert, taking notes and getting his mind ready for the game. That knowledge was not only key to his performance, but also those around him—both players and coaches.

As a rookie, I remember getting the playbook and thinking it looked like an old school phonebook! How could anybody be expected to remember all of that? Most people think being a professional athlete is all about practice and play. But the truth is, it's so much more than that. You need a high IQ to play the game at that level. You have to know the terminology. Studying is necessary to be effective. If you don't get an assignment right or if you bust a play, you could possibly be released. They can find someone else within a day. It's those minor details that separate the best from the rest. The exceptional players pay attention to those small details. Once I was also able to capitalize on those little details that used to seem so minimal—that's when I had an edge.

As I look back over it, the players were fast, they were strong, they were bigger in the NFL. They were exceptional athletes. They were the best at their positions coming out of their schools. But the biggest difference was the mental aspect. Chess instead of checkers. As a young player, that mental execution was what you had to really deal with. And once you were able to settle in mentally, then you could go out and perform as if you were in college or in high school. Once you're able to learn the plays and understand the verbiage and the assignments, you'll be amazed of your natural ability to perform.

## FOCUS ON:
## LIKEABILITY

Several years ago, I was invited to a local Houston radio station to participate in a community event that was taking place. My friend, who was an employee, invited me, so I thought it would be a great opportunity to give back and serve. While there, he took me around to meet the staff, DJs, and volunteers.

As we were about to eat lunch, he said, "JJ, I would love for you to meet one of the station directors." I agreed, so we walked over, and he introduced me to her. Within seconds of conversation, she asked me out of the blue, "How would you like to be the Quarterback Reporter for the radio station every Monday during the football season? You can share insights on NFL Sunday's football games and anything else that would encourage the listeners."

It sounded too good to be true, but, immediately, I said, "Yes, I would love to!"

Little did I know how crucial that first impression would be. I believe what helped me was my genuine interaction with her. I was polite, kind, and truly glad to meet her. All of that translated into likeability because, within seconds of talking, she was preparing to offer me a wonderful opportunity.

If you are reading this book right now and are job hunting or wanting to make a good impression with someone, be sure you smile, dress for the occasion, and pay attention to the way you walk and talk. While they might seem minor or even superficial (you should never judge someone's character by the way they smile, dress, or walk!), visual and verbal cues are incredibly important. Don't make others feel inferior when they are in your presence. You might not realize how your presence makes others feel about themselves.

Be sure to acknowledge everyone in the circle the next time you find yourself talking in a group. Offer a compliment and be generous with your time. Your self-worth is not wrapped up in the opinion of others, but your first impression can open the door to a great opportunity.

# FOCUS ON:
# PASSION

When you are passionate about something, your whole demeanor changes. Passion can be seen in appearance, tone of voice, body language, and how someone dresses. Translate this into your world. What are you passionate about? What gets you excited about waking up each day? What would you do for free? What comes easily to you? Answer these questions, and you'll have a path to a lifetime of happiness.

My daughters had a kindergarten teacher that exemplifies all three principles. She embodies the KLP Factor and has been a true gift to our children and us, as a family. She is knowledgeable and is always providing us with information that goes over and above what we expect. She works with her students in such a way that brings the best out of them. From our first introduction as new parents of elementary kids, we immediately felt at ease and trusted her with our children. She has that immediate likeability factor because she is relatable, understanding, and always available with a friendly disposition. Our kids have excelled in her class because that's truly her aim and focus.

When I first arrived in the NFL, it felt like a foreign land. Everything was more complex. If playing in college was like checkers, then the NFL is chess. Everything is calculated, everything is detailed, everything has a reason. A cause and a reason. I remember walking in and thinking, wow, this is an actual business. It's not always "family"-related. It's driven by performance and the question: what have you done lately for this ball club? It was putting on your big boy pants. Not one minute was wasted. It was nonstop. From meetings to practice, then film, then study, then back to practice. You are at the facility all day long, usually from 6:30 a.m. until 6:30 p.m. You spend more time with the coaches and your teammates than you do with your friends and family. I would never even see the sunrise or the sunset. In that environment, if you don't have the love or the passion for the game, it's going be difficult to stick around.

After my NFL days were over, I didn't know what to do next. I had spent my entire life playing football. It was my life and a fundamental part of my identity. What would come of me without the sport?

I feel so blessed to not have forced a career or hobby. Instead, I took a moment and realized I simply had to discover what it was I wanted to do next. I continued to stay connected to Christ and, by doing this, He brought out talents I didn't know I had. Once a person discovers their gifts and taps into them, passion takes over and leads them to those dream opportunities they are waiting for. For me, it was public speaking. Using that stage to motivate and inspire others with my story gave me a feeling of fulfilment I had never found on the football field.

Still, I wasn't always comfortable speaking in front of crowds. In fact, my first experience was terrifying. As a freshman in high school, I was at the end-of-year football banquet when the coach/counselor invited me to speak on behalf of the football team. Talk about terror? Worse yet, when nervous, I stuttered. So, of course, I had no interest. But my counselor, Mr. Sheeley, took me aside and said something I'll never forget.

"JJ, you might as well get used to this because you will be speaking in front of a lot of people one day."

That one sentence has stayed with me ever since. One line of encouragement was all it took for me to find my lifelong passion.

Isn't it so energizing when you speak to someone passionate about what they do? Whether it's the product they sell, the place in life they are in, or their role as a parent—just being around passion can be inspiring by itself. Passion sells. Passion attracts. Ask yourself: in your job, how does your passion for the job translate each day? Do you bring positivity? Do you energize those around you? Are you so excited about what you do that it makes others stop and take notice? Sometimes we can miss opportunities because we show too little passion. So, the next time a great first impression needs to be made, muster all the passion you possibly can.

# STEP 16.

# RECRUIT YOUR "DREAM TEAM"

I can still remember the anticipation of turning on the TV to catch Team USA's basketball games during the 1992 Olympic Games. For the first time, the squad was made up of NBA players. They were a motley crew of some of the most famous people to ever grace a court and were appropriately labeled "the Dream Team." The roster consisted of Charles Barkley, Magic Johnson, Chris Mullin, John Stockton, Karl Malone, Clyde Drexler, Michael Jordan, Scottie Pippen, Larry Bird, Patrick Ewing, David Robinson, and Christian Laettner.

Not only did the Dream Team win, but they also dominated each game by an average of forty-four points. After securing a gold medal in Barcelona, eleven players and three coaches were inducted into the Naismith Memorial Hall of Fame. The Dream Team was formed from different races, different skill sets, different ages, different walks of life and different experiences, but had one common goal—victory.

This is a model that we can all copy to create our own "Dream Team." Success is determined by whom you associate with, so it is vital to pick your friends as if you were a scout for the 1992 men's Olympic basketball team. The saying "iron sharpens iron" implies that there is a benefit from interacting with other firm and challenging people. Polyester or cotton doesn't sharpen iron. To be as sharp as you can be, engage with others who not only support you, but also refuse to let you get away with giving anything less than what you are capable of. They hold you accountable, and that constant interaction should make for a relentless sharpening of skills.

Leading up to my senior year at Iowa State, I took a long hard look at myself to make sure I was still being sharpened, in a sense. I knew it was vital for me to surround myself with people who pushed me. I wanted to finish my senior year strong and be in the best position possible to get some attention from the NFL. My first three years went by incredibly fast and, to be honest, I felt that I might have wasted certain opportunities. To get to that next level, I knew I needed people who would inspire and hold me accountable. I wanted to surround myself with a Dream Team.

I changed my roommate situation and moved in with a friend that I had greatly respected. This guy was always giving it his all, was on time, persistent, and looking for ways in which he could work harder. He was legendary on our campus and earned the nickname "Mammal" because it was always apparent that he was going to outwork anyone and everyone. He was eventually drafted to play for the Arizona Cardinals.

Just by being around him, I knew his work ethic would change me—if only through a kind of osmosis. I had gone from a student who was late for early morning practices and warm-ups to arriving early with Mammal and ending my runs feeling accomplished, convinced I had given it all I had.

Our team had a 9–3 record that season, which remains one of the best records in school history, and was the first winning season in ten years. We led Iowa State to its first Bowl game in twenty-two years. Finding my Dream Team was the key to not only an unforgettable season, but also signing with the Kansas City Chiefs.

Who do you associate with at work, at school, and when you're just hanging out? Who are the friends in your inner circle—do you all encourage each other to excel? Decisions like this are vital to becoming a person who achieves their goals.

During my life, I've had the opportunity to team up with people who brought out the best in each other and also those who were toxic. I have found that at an elite level, Dream Team members always have the following traits that lift up everyone around them.

## FOCUS ON:
## RESPECTING OTHERS

Respecting your coworkers and boss sounds easy enough until you are slammed with extra work, tight due dates, late emails, incessant calls, and unexpected challenges. Maintaining respect for yourself and others—regardless of the environment—will bring out the power of a team. It's easy to get comfortable with a boss or coworker you see every day but maintaining respect for their position is important to the health of your team and company.

# FOCUS ON:
# PURPOSEFUL LISTENING

Good teammates listen to each other. The ones that seem like they are just waiting for you to pause so they can tell you about themselves are showing their priorities. Check yourself and slow down. Let people talk. Remember to pass the ball as we'd say on the field. And, of course, try not to talk unless you have something to contribute. Remember, it's better to remain silent and be thought a fool than to speak and remove all doubt.

I heard the story of two prime ministers in Victorian-era England running against each other. Winston Churchill's mother, Jennie Jerome, had the opportunity to dine with both men, William Gladstone and Benjamin Disraeli. When it came to Gladstone, she was incredibly impressed with how smart, talented, and clever he was. After dining with Disraeli, however, she was impressed with how smart, talented, and clever he made *her* feel. Who do you think won that year?

By truly listening, Disraeli mastered the art of listening and was able to bring out the greatness in others, and greatness continued to follow him.

## FOCUS ON:
# COMPASSION AND EMPATHY

Be mindful of others around you. You don't have be best friends with everyone, but a simple hello, eye contact, and smile speak volumes about who you are as a person. Genuine kindness and friendliness will never be outdated. People skills are the best skills to take to the pro level! That's because winning cultures always establish healthy lines of communication. Team members should understand the chain of command and the flow of communication. Introduction of new staff members is important so that they are not left to figure things out on their own and the existing staff are aware of who they are and what their role on their team is. Managers should be accessible to team members so that, as needs arise, team members can ask questions, problem solve, and resolve issues in a timely manner. Encourage time sensitivity on replying to phone calls, emails, or follow ups from meetings. Nothing stunts a productive workday more than lingering to-do lists that cannot be accomplished because of a delay in communication.

# FOCUS ON:
## PATIENCE AND PROGRESS

When the prophet Zechariah has a vision of a lampstand and two olive trees—which represent the rebuilding of the Temple in Jerusalem—the angel says the task in front of them will not be easy but can be accomplished through the power of God. Zechariah, in turn, tells the people of Israel, "do not despise the days of small beginnings," hoping to save them from feeling discouraged by the seemingly insignificant progress that was being made in the reconstruction. Instead, they should have faith in God's plan and understand that even tiny steps, taken in the right direction, can lead to great things in the future. The lesson is simple but vital: great things often have humble beginnings and progress. Growth and development is a gradual process.

The same message can be applied to how teams develop. Chemistry might not always be there from day one. The process can sometimes be slow and even painful, but small improvements should be celebrated.

Arranging team building activities is an easy and obvious way to help you learn more about staff members and for them to learn more about you. These activities do not have to be extravagant. They can range from simple games, to challenges, to team dinners, and I have seen them work wonders for NFL teams all the way to church volunteer groups.

# FOCUS ON:
## BEING RESPECTFUL OF PEOPLE AND PLACE

Where you put yourself as a leader in your workspace can build team sensibility. I remember watching a coach walk through a room, see trash on the floor, and then go out of his way to pick it up and put it in the garbage can. That told me so much about him, his approach and place on the team. Similarly, in my years of working within the National Football League, I took notice of how players kept their lockers. After the last World Cup, a video went viral of the Japanese team that cleaned up after themselves, left a thank-you message, and gifted origami cranes to the locker room staff.

I don't have scientific data to back this theory, but, in my time in the NFL, I saw a correlation between players who were organized, precise, and intentional with their lockers and workspaces and how they executed at a higher level on the field.

# STEP 17.

# THREE PILLARS OF POSITIVE LEADERSHIP

B eing positive naturally leads to sharing positivity. It's like walking around with a flashlight—you can't help but unintentionally shine it in people's directions all the time. And think of this—have you ever meet anybody who horded their positivity? Impossible! You have positivity, you are going to leak positivity all over the place.

Positivity is a powerful tool in leadership, as it can have a significant impact on the mindset and motivation of those being led. When leaders exude positivity, it creates a positive and supportive work environment. This can foster a culture of trust, collaboration, and open communication, which are all, of course, key ingredients for a successful team. A positive leader also sets an example for the team to follow, encouraging them to approach their work and challenges with an optimistic attitude. This can not only lead to a reduction in conflicts, stress, and burnout, but also increased resilience in the team. When faced with difficult situations, a positive leader helps team members to maintain a positive outlook, encouraging them to focus on solutions and opportunities rather than problems. This can help the team to bounce back quickly from setbacks and continue to move forward. Moreover, positive people tend to be more creative, productive, effective problem solvers—not to mention better collaborators and more effective communicators. Therefore, a positive leader can help the team to develop these skills and become more effective in their roles.

As one of the "Prepare to Win" program's most important messages, I organized the skill into the following three sections.

## FOCUS ON:
## POSITIVE COMMUNICATION

Do your best to create an atmosphere that encourages high levels of positive communication. When done right, this puts people in a zone that makes them feel secure, which, in turn, will make them more likely to offer creative ideas and pitch in with solutions to seemingly intractable problems. A positive atmosphere will also drastically increase productivity when compared to a space filled with negative communication.

How can you help create a positive communication zone? Be aware of the people around you and offer help and encouragement, or even a compassionate comment. Recognizing accomplishments, birthdays, and personal wins within the group will let people know they are part of a supportive unit. We all need feedback, so work on ways to provide it in a way that is constructive and not with harsh criticism. For every criticism offered, try to find two things a person is doing right.

Being prompt in returning phone messages and emails shows consideration and respect. Even if you don't have the time to answer, let the person know that their message has been received and that you will be in touch soon. Timely responses are a great way to cultivate positive relationships in the workplace.

Positive communication also includes your body language. We pick up a lot more than we are consciously aware of. Wear a perpetual scowl, cross your arms, and glare at people, and they are not going to feel welcome to interact with you. It means a lot to greet people by name so do that while recognizing that the tone of voice and bounce in your step conveys your approach to life.

In team meetings, players that came in slouching down in chairs or not engaged in the meetings had a tougher time emerging as leaders than players that came into the room focused, attentive, and engaged. Make no mistake! Coaches and staff are always studying players' nonverbal communications, and it influences their decisions on a player's future. It's the same with any good boss looking at his staff in the workplace.

One rule I practiced is that regardless of what was happening at home or on the job, I never allowed it to negatively impact how I presented myself. I told myself I would deal with it later, because there was nothing I could do at the time. I wasn't going to drag it around with me. I learned that just by holding myself in a physically open and welcoming manner made me feel better.

# FOCUS ON:
# FOSTERING POSITIVE RELATIONSHIPS

All healthy relationships start with trust. If you reach out to pet a dog and he bites you, you are not going to trust him the next time you see him. Confidentiality is a very common word, but in today's workplace betraying it can be like that dog bite. If you have sensitive information or an individual confides in you, establish trust by maintaining confidentiality. Give them your word and teach them about your character by keeping their trust.

Another way to have positive relationships is by providing support that goes above and beyond. Show partners and people around you that they have potential and help them achieve goals that they never thought they were capable of. It's relationships like these that build people's confidence. And when people become energized to challenge themselves, they almost always help others do the same, so there is a chain reaction that can change a negative zone into a positive one.

Recognize when someone has made a big win even if it doesn't affect you. Take notice. When people drift into negativity and try to frame positivity as a weakness, tell them how it's, actually, a major strength. Don't hold back in that regard. The Dallas Cowboys owner Jerry Jones once said, "I do my best work when it's more positive. When I hear people tell me I'm naïve? Well, it's a *beautiful* world and it's a better world to be naïve in than to be skeptical and negative all the time."

Know from the outset that some people see being positive as simple-minded or as a weakness. That is their problem, not yours. Sometimes your positivity will be met with aggression and bullying.

We may spend a lot of time with people at work, but, at the end of the day, it's a job. Treat others with respect, boundaries, and consideration. In a sense, many of us are in jobs that can feel like we're perpetually in those last few pre-season games waiting to see who gets cut and who makes the roster. Don't give the decision-makers any reason to put you on the cut list.

# FOCUS ON:
## SUSTAINING POSITIVE WORK CULTURES

The American Psychological Association estimates that more than $500 billion is siphoned off from the U.S. economy because of workplace stress, and 550 million workdays are lost each year due to stress on the job. Also, 60–80 percent of workplace accidents are attributed to stress, and it's estimated that more than 80 percent of doctors' visits are due to stress. Well, that was a pile of bad news, but there is one positive aspect—look how we can improve the situation!

A culture of high pressure is the worst atmosphere an organization can encourage. An environment of positivity, on the other hand, can prepare your organization to succeed in ways you could only imagine. Be intentional about positivity in the workplace and see how it improves a person's ability to bounce back from difficult situations or defeats. People around you will feel valued instead of just a number in your system. No one wants to dread going into work or having to deal with another person.

I look at work not only as a place that issues you a check. School, church, community centers, football teams are all places of work in my mind, regardless of whether they provide income or not. So, perhaps most valuable of all, we need to teach our children these lessons. My children had the privilege of attending a wonderful school that was under the leadership of a principal who exemplified so many ways of winning. The school has received straight A's for progress, student achievement (how well students perform over time compared to students in similar schools), and for closing the gaps (how well schools are boosting performance for subgroups such as students with special needs).

The principal had over twenty years of experience at the school as a teacher, counselor, and assistant principal, and she was well aware of the power of positivity and how it worked at all levels of the school experience. She won the Excellence in Leadership Award for her exceptional leadership after Hurricane Harvey. Her positive communication skills were always on display when kids arrived and left school each day.

Organizations take on the temperature of their leadership. Create a positive space and reap the benefits of higher productivity, creative output, and overall happiness.

# STEP 18.

## KNOWING THE DIFFERENCE BETWEEN SECURE AND INSECURE LEADERSHIP

All of us have been exposed to a variety of leadership styles. I've had coaches that scream and bully to try and make players perform at a higher level. There have also been bosses that listen to everybody's input and make them feel like a part of the decision-making process.

Being on so many NFL teams, I witnessed leadership executed at a very high level. One of the perks of my pro career was being able to experience so many styles of authority and the results those styles had on different personality types. The most amazing experience was when you saw a player develop from follower to leader.

Operating from a position of leadership can be tricky at times. Many of us see ourselves using the gifts we have been given to inspire, encourage, and elevate those around us. However, be careful what you wish for. Every leader knows that it is impossible to please everyone when decisions have to be made. To be in leadership, you need to be comfortable with unpopularity and free yourself from the burden of making everyone happy.

But leading can come naturally for all of us—not just in government and corporate settings, but also in our homes, our schools, our circles of influence, and our communities. For me, the most effective leaders openly value others and consider it their job to show the others what they could achieve. Inspirational coaches treat people as individuals—not just numbers on a uniform—and value the experiences each person brings to the team. They aren't competitive with those they are leading and will even lean on them to help solve problems.

The proof of a strong leader is how they recognize differences but masterfully bring everyone together for a common purpose. Insecure leaders want to control the environment. There is an old saying: "If it isn't broken, then don't fix it." If you're in a leadership position, then I want to challenge you with a new quote: "If it isn't broken, then break it." Simply meaning, think outside the box and become more open-minded.

Harvard Business Review found that diverse teams are able to solve problems faster than cognitively similar people. McKinsey & Company, a global management consulting firm, conducted research that included companies in France, Germany, the United Kingdom, and the United States. Guess what? The companies with more diversity were top financial performers.

My best coaches were always secure leaders. They empowered others by giving them the freedom to make decisions. They fostered collaborative environments, which, in turn, put more responsibility on the individual. If the coach pointed to a play and told me to cut here, run this way and then that way, all I had do was follow his pattern. Not so if the coach said, "JJ, there might be a hole in the defense on the fifty-yard line, but they also have a habit of spreading their special teams too thin when the ball is kicked deeper than expected. I want you to see what is happening and either get through the hole or see if you can thin them out even more and find an opening."

He's still the coach, still calling the play, but one requires no personal leadership from me, while the other demands I still employ the same skill set while taking ownership over my performance. Ideally, team members know they are responsible, but also know they have the support of their leader. The strongest leaders hire and promote others who think differently than they do. They aren't intimidated by somebody knowing more than them or being more skilled in a particular department. They see leadership as a team sport. Why not pack the team with as much skill as possible? Steve Jobs had the right idea when he said, "It doesn't make sense to hire smart people and tell them what to do. We hire smart people so they can tell us what to do."

I've seen so many insecure people in leadership roles purposely recruit weaker and less talented people. It's an insecure strategy that guarantees nobody else on the team can outshine them. When your team is stacked with people skilled in unique ways, your team becomes greater than the sum of their parts. Creating that kind of situation is secure leadership.

The best leaders build a team that demonstrates care. They are sensitive to the emotional temperature of their team. They surround themselves with people who never stop learning and are eager for new, challenging experiences. This naturally leads to a crew that encourages growth for everybody they manage. The heart of any proficient team is a belief that everybody can exceed their own expectations. Diversity can be a word that people can dilute, but a good leader gets sparked by having a wide range of experiences around to help him or her miss any blind spots. There is nothing more fatal to a group bond than when a person doesn't accept responsibility for a mistake, and this has to be modeled from the top down.

Regardless of somebody's experience, the insecure leader knows it all—nobody can trump their expertise. They overreact and not only throw suspicion and accusations around frivolously but are also quick to point fingers and aim blame when there is a problem. Gossip and division define the environment of a toxic leader. The emotionally polluted atmosphere is constantly electrified with chaos and dysfunction, which, naturally, is not the leader's fault—they'll find somebody else to blame.

# STEP 19.

# BE A FIRE LIGHTER, NOT A FIRE FIGHTER

S urrounding yourself with winners depends on being able to identify positive traits in people—the ones who bring out the best in those around them. Unfortunately, that also means being able to sense when someone is trying to do the opposite. To make it easier, I developed categories for each extreme—fire lighters and fire fighters.

Fire lighters are those who have something positive to say every time they see you—they radiate warmth and spark an internal flame with everybody they meet. Compliments come off these people like glowing embers from a bonfire. Positivity comes so naturally and so honestly that you cannot help but admire the way they see the world. They can pick a silver lining out of what others see as a disaster and immediately stoke constructive action.

These people speak the language of the heart and find ways to remind you of the dreams you are chasing. They see your possibilities and naturally find ways to help you seek them out.

I played basketball in high school. But as I only stood 5'6", most people saw my height as a disadvantage. I'm sure all of us can recall when someone in a position of authority—a supposed expert—highlighted what they considered your deficit. I had a basketball coach who even called me "midget."

Why a coach, who is in charge of getting the most out of his players, would choose to highlight and make fun of what he saw as a negative says more about his personality than my genetics. Was I going to be able to change my height? He could have found ways to help improve my jump shot or point guard skills, but he chose instead to mock what he saw as a handicap.

Sure, my height was an easy target for teasing, but I've found that we all have characteristics of ourselves that we feel insecure about at one time or another. We're all made uniquely and if you're a fire lighter, then you find ways to empower those differences. The key is to not bully your-self, but, instead, break apart what others categorize as a deficit and use creativity, effort, and determination to maximize your uniqueness.

I already had a sense of my self-worth by the time I was called a "midget" by my basketball coach. Whether it was a joke or he had intended to intimidate me, I didn't allow his words to influence my personal think-ing. I had learned to be very careful about who was allowed into my circle of influence because I didn't want negative energy to drain my focus. In my eyes, I was tall enough—and that was all that mattered. I carried myself with the confidence of a 6'2" player. Those eight added inches might not have shown up in a mirror, but I felt them in the faith I had in myself. When you get a good coach, a good friend, a solid supporter—whoever they are—you feel the added momentum of their belief in you, especially when compared to those always looking for reasons to see you fail.

During my first year in the NFL, I was thankful to have head coach Dick Vermeil, who was a professional fire lighter. Over and over, I watched him draw out an inner source of power in others that they had never seen in themselves. He brought out the potential in players that they didn't know they had. And he was the kind of man who did this to everybody—not just players, but coaches and staff too. Once somebody shows you a hidden ember of potential, all you have to do is start blowing on it until the flame inside you ignites.

It's no surprise that Coach Vermeil is so beloved, not to mention a Super Bowl Champion. He's also been Coach of the Year on four levels: High School, Junior College, NCAA Division I and the NFL. In 2022, he was inducted into the NFL Hall of Fame. So many players he coached went on to have elite careers and just as many others talk about how he taught them how to win off the field. Much more than just a coach, he is a mentor and father figure in a totally selfless way. He showed me the joy that comes from lighting fires in others.

Fire *fighters* on the other hand are individuals who compulsively find ways to stomp out the inner fires of others. Out of insecurity, to deal with their failings, they throw water on any sparks in their vicinity. They can't find an encouraging thing to say and intuitively zero in on a perceived negative. It's as if they're pro at finding ways that life won't work. Sometimes their ability to tease out a negative in a situation is simply amazing—like the kind of people who focus on the taxes after hearing someone won the lottery. They are expert at figuring out all the reasons why things won't work out for you.

Fire fighters typically view the world from the perspective of having low self-esteem and lack of confidence because they were not willing to go after their dreams. If they can convince themselves that nobody around them succeeds in chasing their dreams, then it's obviously not their fault, right? Instead of learning from failure, they live in a mindset that encourages them to repeat what doesn't work. "You were cut from an NFL team, JJ? Well, you're always going to be too short." "Playing ball in this part of the country isn't going to get any looks from scouts." "Dang, no wonder you got cut after playing a game like that."

If I had taken their advice and hadn't dug through my "losses" for opportunity, then I never would have helped my friend by catching balls at his NFL tryout, which changed my life. Fire fighters are incapable of seeing the positives in a situation but remember that the world is full of fire lighters. Remember how I told you I was cut from a team and then got a call to come play for the team that I lost to? Coaches of the opposing team that intuitively looked for the positives in my play are prime examples of fire lighters.

You must be very careful about even casually hanging out with fire fighters. The more successful people think you are, the more aggressive their fire stomping becomes. After I was let go from an NFL team, I went home and got together with some friends to play pool. As I was about to take a shot, an individual we knew walked over to me and exclaimed, "JJ, you got released from another NFL team! Out of thirty-two teams, you don't have talent for at least one of them to want you?"

Wow! My first reaction was, this guy is tripping! His comments stung, but why would a person walk out of his way to say something like that to another person? He had never even been noticed by a professional team, so he could have come over and talked about how amazing it must have felt to have had a dream come true and play on an NFL team, even if it was brief. How many people get that opportunity in their lives? Instead, he stomped down to make sure that all the embers of somebody else's dream were completely extinguished.

But people like this guy and other fire fighters can never extinguish your dreams and sense of self-worth—only you can do that. Always remember that. This was just an individual at a pool hall and didn't have any agency over my life. I had to deal with a coach who was in charge of letting me play, and that guy called me midget. I knew a fire fighter when I saw one and ignored his comments.

A few weeks after this pool hall diss, I was picked up by another NFL team. I had stayed in pro ball shape and was ready to strike when they called because I didn't listen to some fire fighter in a pool hall. Unfortunately, the world is full of fire fighters, and they might be a coworker, boss, classmate, or teammate. You must learn to ignore them and continue to be your best. Use their negative outlook as a warning.

No matter how "successful" you get in life, even when you think you are in a zone devoid of fire fighters, they have a tendency to pop up. Early on in my pro football career, the team got on a plane. We all found our seats and settled in for a long flight. An assistant coach was making the rounds and found his way over to me and we started talking. He said casually, "JJ, the only way you are going to play in the NFL is if this plane crashes and there are no survivors."

Holy smokes! Why would you say that? At the very least, having come from a culture of firelighters, I knew why this guy was one of the numerous "assistant" coaches. Going out of your way to drop one of the coldest things a member of a coaching staff could say to a young player is not going to motivate *anybody* on the team. Of course, I understood the odds were stacked against me by being an undrafted player that stood 5'6", but what exactly was the point of his comments? Regardless, if I was not sure of my self-worth, then I might have been in serious trouble.

Be very diligent about fortifying your own sense of self so it will be unshaken by other supposed "experts." Don't let the watchmaker shortchange you because they see a few scratches! I could have believed what the assistant coach said, but I knew God didn't bring me this far to let someone else's negative opinion steer my future. I wonder if this guy even noticed or reflected on the impact of his words when I persevered and became a starter and then played for nearly five years, which is almost twice as long as the average career? I'm not thinking this out of any sort of revenge; rather, that it might make him think about what he says to the next player trying to battle odds on a team flight.

And, thank God, no one had to die in an airplane crash for me to play!

Take some time and reflect on the people in your life. Meditate over their support and encouragement and make sure you surround yourself and spend most of your time with people excited to see the fire within you glowing.

# STEP 20.

# NEVER FORGET THE POWER OF WORDS

Whoever coined the phrase "sticks and stones will break my bones, but words will never hurt me" clearly never tried to make it in the NFL at 5'6".

Words are powerful and, like any weapon, can be wielded to cause maximum damage. Trust me, I've heard it all. While I was taught to see bullying or taunts as a reflection of the person throwing them, it's still impossible to fully avoid the sting. Dr. Hyder Zahed captured the sentiment perfectly when he said "words are singularly the most powerful force available to humanity. Words have energy and power with the ability to help, to heal, to hinder, to hurt, to harm, to humiliate, and to humble."

With that in mind, my mom always repeated the old saying "Give them their flowers when they are still living." Even as a kid, I was encouraged to speak or share good things about someone *now*, not later—when it's too late. Let others hear how they are positively impacting your life, in the moment and whenever possible. You might assume they already know how you feel, or you might be too embarrassed to verbally express something so "mushy," but, I can tell you from experience, that people open up in surprising ways when you tell them how much they mean to you.

If you've ever been around a dying loved one, you know how important this lesson can be. Treat every minute like that because life is short, and nothing is guaranteed. When I look back over my career, I see so many moments when positive words gave me the confidence needed to keep moving forward. To keep working toward the lofty goals I might have otherwise doubted were within my grasp.

For example, I will never forget my fifth-grade teacher.

Mrs. Brace, who always commented on my optimism, nicknamed me "Mr. Positive." Now, in elementary school, I never knew I was *that* positive, but her words inspired me to live up to the moniker. So, I focused even harder on being that type of person. For my kid brain, it was more like a job title. I was like a little boxing champ focused on not losing my title belt.

As a result, the name stayed with me into my adulthood. As I grew up and my perspective widened, I saw the blast radius of being positive and how vital a proper attitude was to overcome the obstacles I inevitably faced. Positivity, in other words, was a built-in generator for progress, for development, for growth. It was a key that unlocked all the powers within us for self-improvement.

Do not ever underestimate the power of your positive words. Whether you're in a leadership position or not, your voice can impact the lives of those around you. Even in your darkest moments, words can be a form of light. They can pick someone up when the weight of the world seems like it is on their shoulders. As the Bible says: "Life and death are in the power of your words."

Also, keep in mind that, as we age, we change. We've all heard about party animals who were devastated by social anxiety as kids; the chronically shy children who blossomed into stand-up comedians; the high school dropouts who became billionaire tech entrepreneurs. Often this personality pivot can be attributed to someone believing in them during their most difficult moments and conveying that belief through words.

My parents, certainly, had their hands full with my childhood shyness. To help break me out of my shell, they signed me up for the local Boys and Girls Club—where I'd go at least three times a week to play basketball. While there, slowly, my confidence began to grow as I interacted and competed with other kids. During this time, I began to receive positive affirmations from the club's staff. As the shortest kid on the court, their compliments were instrumental in helping me develop a competitive edge and a sense of confidence in my athletic abilities. As a matter of fact, they helped me see my size as an advantage. One less foot of height meant one less foot of mass that could be used to hold me back.

The power of the positive affirmations has been a force in my life ever since, even in other competitions where height wasn't as much of a deciding factor. For example, my hometown held an annual bike race, which I, in hindsight, might have been a bit too competitive about. As a kid, I was the kind of rider with my tongue coming out from the corners of my mouth while the bike swayed violently from side to side—my entire being pushing into each thrust of the pedal. With that kind of intensity, you might not be shocked to learn that I won the race, year after year.

Still, I feel like every one of those medals belongs to my older brother Clayton, who convinced me I could *actually* win.

"JJ, you can do it," he'd say. "You have what it takes."

Like a laser, he'd focus his positive energy into me. With him by my side, I didn't feel any shorter than the tallest competitor in the race. The way he explained it to me, losing just wasn't possible and, if I didn't cross that finish line first, it was because I wasn't pushing hard enough. Not because someone else was better, stronger, or faster than me. With that kind of mindset, you'll at least cross the finish of the race with no regrets—and that is, always, more important than winning.

Sometimes, though, positivity can be delivered in less obvious ways. When I was in elementary school, my Aunt Jewell gave me a personalized Bible for Christmas. Honestly, a Bible was *not* on my wish list because I wanted the latest toy or video game. Still, she had this unyielding confidence when she said, "this will be the most important gift you will ever receive."

Those words planted a seed of faith in my heart that continues to grow to this day. Indeed, the Bible—and the message she passed along when gifting it—laminated another layer of confidence within, one that is impervious to any negative or hurtful language directed my way.

If you ever find yourself lacking a mentor, teacher, or parent to lean on for support, open a Bible. The words within will give you whatever nourishment, confidence and focus your soul is seeking.

# STEP 21.

## SPREZZATURA AND THE ANCIENT ART OF MAKING HARD THINGS LOOK EFFORTLESS

W e've all seen them. People overflowing with charisma, charm, and style, yet embodying a kind of energy that makes their swagger seem effortless. It might not come as a surprise that the Italians have a word for this phenomenon: sprezzatura. *Merriam-Webster* defines it as "studied nonchalance: graceful conduct or performance without apparent effort," and the term dates all the way back to *The Book of the Courtier*, written by Baldassare Castiglione in the early sixteenth century. During the Renaissance, "sprezzatura" was seen as an important quality for those who operated in society's upper crust. It was suggested that the most effective way to demonstrate one's level of education, sophistication, and mastery of various skills was by making it all seem completely effortless.

In the modern world, the concept tends to be applied in the realm of fashion, often used to describe an outfit that appears to be easily put together yet, in reality, is the result of careful planning and attention to detail. Someone who embodies sprezzatura might mix high- and low-end items in a seemingly haphazard way, even though every single aspect has been thought out and executed with precision. On a more metaphysical level, however, sprezzatura represents a kind of confidence and self-assurance that reflects inner strength and grace. Or, in other words, a winning and focused mindset.

Think of the dancer who worked on the same movement for hours but, when it's time to be on the stage in front of the world, makes the steps look incredibly easy. In the workplace, sprezzatura can refer to the ability to make even the most complex tasks appear simple and effortless. It can also refer to the way in which we represent ourselves in a professional setting, with a balance of confidence, humility, and grace. In the sports arena, sprezzatura is embodied by athletes who win championships seemingly with ease. In the art and design world, sprezzatura is the ideal balance between pragmatism and aesthetics, like that perfect piece of furniture that is both beautiful and comfortable. It can be felt in relationships, too. In such cases, sprezzatura would be personified by individuals who are able to communicate effectively and handle social situations effortlessly, making even the most difficult conversations seem natural.

During my playing days, whenever I scored a touchdown, my dad told me to act like I had been in the endzone before. Sure, he didn't want me showboating, spiking the ball, or making it about me. But what he was really telling me is that I shouldn't be caught up with my success, a motto I've taken with me in all aspects of my life. It's just so easy to let success go to your head. In fact, winning can be a double-edged sword: it can give you a sense of accomplishment and a heavy dose of self-esteem, but it can also lead to dangerous consequences—like arrogance and entitlement.

I bet you've witnessed it before. Someone gets on a hot streak, they start to feel superior to others, and then their relationships become strained, leading eventually to social isolation. Remember, too, that success triggers increased stress and pressure, because, for certain individuals, as they become more successful, they begin to sense the need to maintain that level of success. It's a perfect recipe for burnout and other mental health issues such as anxiety and depression. And then, in others, I've seen success blaze a trail toward complacency. It can stifle motivation and creativity as well as increase the likelihood of stagnation in both personal and professional realms. Indeed, success can distort your sense of perspective and lead to a form of narrow-mindedness that can negatively impact friendships and long-term personal growth. So, stay humble and carry your wins with a sense of sprezzatura. As my dad would say, act like you've been there before.

Years ago, I was flying back to Iowa for an event. My brother Milan was picking me up from the airport in Cedar Rapids, Iowa, and, as I was putting my bags in the car, I noticed the cologne he had on smelled so clean I had no choice but to ask him which brand it was. He immediately started laughing and said, "Man, I forgot what this even is, I've had it on all day." Later, however, I learned he had applied it just before pulling up to the airport! What would my reaction have been to the scent if the first thing he did was open the door and show off his new cologne? Would I have appreciated it in the same way? I doubt it.

My brother was practicing sprezzatura years ago, without even knowing it.

I'm not endorsing lying or putting on a front, to be sure. The story simply highlights a simple truth: the best way to get attention is to not seek it. When you look desperate, people will see desperation and respond negatively. For example, when you are single and act like anyone filling that void in your life is better than nobody, you might settle for a relationship that is not best for you. But once you are comfortable with who you are and your independence, the right relationship will find you. If you're job hunting and reach out to a hiring manager, begging for a position because no one else will hire you, then that manager will think there is a reason no one else is interested—even if there aren't any other explanations for why you wouldn't be a good candidate. However, if you reach out to that same hiring manager with a sense of confidence and competence, you'll have a much better chance of landing an interview. Remember, confidence suggests competence.

As an NFL punt returner, I had to act calm and loose under an immense amount of pressure. When I was holding the ball, I felt like I was carrying not only my team in my arms but also both the entire city and the livelihoods of those in the organization's front office. In addition, I was always on the bubble of not making the roster, so every single play counted. Preseason was especially tough. It was raging hot, fiercely competitive, and mentally taxing. A teammate once said something I'll never forget: "Training camp is where the strong get weak, but the weak shall die." If I hadn't embodied a sprezzatura mindset, I'm not convinced the coaches would have had the confidence in me that they did. I would have been one of the weak whose football dreams would have "died" and evaporated in the August heat.

Can you look opposition in the face and not back down? Can you handle your emotions if your company decides to downsize or you lose a loved one? Can you keep your zeal? Your sprezzatura? Let me encourage you, now. This last step is vital to your success, because when people sense your confidence, they will have confidence in you. And when the rest of your team or group has confidence in you, you'll gain even more confidence in yourself. It's an energizing cycle. The reverse is also true. If you're in a leadership position, and your reports see that you're not thriving, they too will have trouble being successful. Again, I'm not endorsing that you repress your feelings or deny them to other people—or even yourself. Don't fake it 'til you make it. Instead, *faith* it 'til you make it. Have confidence in God's plan for you. That doesn't mean you can just sit around waiting for God to do everything. But if you show God that you're willing to work toward the dream or goal, I believe God will deliver it.

The only way to survive, then, is to sometimes *try* and swim—even if you don't know how. I once asked a successful business owner for her most important single piece of advice when it came to starting a company. She said never turn down an opportunity, even if you don't know how to do the job. Fear could be all that is standing between you and the chance of a lifetime.

Not letting fear or insecurity dictate your outward energy is of the utmost importance in your personal life as well. Take being a parent, for example. There are times when you are not always at your best, you are depleted and feeling like you have nothing more to give, but, when duty calls and your child needs you to show up for them, the sprezzatura will kick in. That's how the most difficult situation can end up feeling effortless, at least to those around you.

Each year, my wife makes sure we send out a family Christmas card to our friends and family. We're always featured with the kids and in our best outfits, looking like we don't have a care in the world. Or at least that's what the final photos look like when the card lands in mailboxes. In actuality, the entire photo shoot is a roller coaster of emotions because the kids have meltdowns for any number of reasons. Sometimes it's because they're hungry; other times they need to use the restroom or want to change into something more comfortable. The most common cause is that they simply don't want to take the picture! As parents, however, we realize this is a sprezzatura moment. We have to have the emotional discipline to not let our environment and those around us dictate our moods and actions. We must take a deep breath, take charge of the moment, and show everyone that the seemingly impossible is entirely possible.

This is not just necessary with the kids, either. My wife loves to plan parties and events. However, over the years of watching her behind the scenes, I question her "love" for party planning. Before the guests arrive, I see the stress and a mad dash to put the party or event together. Her carefully thought-out timetable is behind schedule; there might have been dishes ordered that did not arrive in time or decorations that aren't coming together as planned. But once people arrive and everyone is enjoying themselves, Sarah seems like the calmest one there. As a result, guests end up asking her for advice. Sometimes they even try to recruit her for their own events! Still, after every major holiday or birthday, she vows that her party planning days are over. Yet, without fail, she finds a way to spearhead the next major family event. Now that's sprezzatura in action!

Simply put, sprezzatura makes hard things look easy, and it's one of the most wonderfully infectious and welcoming qualities in a person. Think of a duck on the water. From the shore, we see a sense of calm. The bird gently floating along the surface of a lake. But if you could glimpse beneath the water, you'd see two webbed feet churning tirelessly like pistons. The turmoil of the scene underneath, compared to the serenity above, is sprezzatura. No, life is not always easy, relationships are not always easy, work is not always easy, parenting is not always easy. But when you have the sprezzatura mindset, people will only see you flourishing. You will have embodied a mindset that ensures you'll get the best out of every situation. Here are some helpful ways to overcome the pressure and make things look effortless.

# FOCUS ON:
# THREE TECHNIQUES TO IMPLEMENT
# WHEN YOU FEEL THE PRESSURE

1. Release your feelings: Our instincts can make it easy to hold everything inside, but sprezzatura doesn't mean you can never show vulnerability. Always make sure you have support, whether it's from a friend, mentor, pastor, or counselor.

2. Let go of ego: Sometimes you might worry that no one else is cut out for a certain task, but that feeling can often come from a place of arrogance. Don't be afraid to delegate or share the workload with other individuals on your team.

3. Prioritize your attention: Don't get distracted by the environment around you. We can't always control what's going on in our presence, so be intentional with your focus by concentrating on what demands your attention.

# EPILOGUE

# THE NUMBER 84

Parents can be pillars in our lives. We look up to and learn from them. They are foundational in developing who we are in our most impressionable years.

One of the most powerful things a parent can do is model sacrifice. As a parent, you might have had to put your dreams on hold to provide for your family. Life rarely goes the way any of us plans (this can be a great thing!) and sometimes we use those lessons to instill traits in our children that we wish we had at that age. My dad wanted to play in the National Football League ever since he was young and he chased that dream hard, but injuries and other events derailed that dream.

My dad was on the right track, that's for sure. He was a standout football player at Waterloo East High. He played varsity for three years, helping set the Trojans' fifty-six-game winning streak from 1965 to 1972. The Des Moines Register ran an article on Iowa's greatest all-time prep football players, and he was on that list. From 1968 to 1969, my dad rushed for fifty-six career touchdowns, was twice named to the first team All-State, and was eventually inducted into the Iowa High School Hall of Fame.

His reputation carried into his adult life and, in 2013, *The Des Moines Register* selected my dad as one of Iowa's all-time greatest male athletes, ranking him fifth on a list behind Nile Kinnick, Bob Feller, Gary Thompson, and Dan Gable, who also is a Waterloo native. His scholarship offer count hit the triple digits, as universities like Alabama, Colorado, Notre Dame, Missouri, Iowa, and Nebraska begged my dad to come play for them. College representatives would even fly to Iowa to visit with him. The legendary coach, Bear Bryant, from the University of Alabama, flew to Iowa and visited him as a senior in high school. At the time, Alabama was arguably the dream school for any football player to attend.

While the invitation was an honor, my dad felt like Alabama was too far from home. So, after careful consideration, and several meetings with various colleges, he chose to attend Iowa State University. University of Iowa was going through a coaching change and hadn't named their head coach yet, so he chose Iowa State because of Johnny Majors, a promising young leader who would go on to become a Hall of Fame Division I coach.

Unfortunately, my dad had little impact on his college football team. Injury after injury plagued him, and he was sidelined for most of his career at Iowa State. It was a special kind of disappointment to have the will and the spirit but to feel the body lacking. As an athlete, you know your body, so you also know, very specifically, when it begins to fail. Your legs, lungs, and back might be in prime shape, but if you have foot problems or a torn ACL, then your leg is not going to be stable enough to pivot from.

After his playing days at Iowa State, he decided to try out for the National Football League, specifically for the Houston Oilers. He always dreamed of playing in Houston and at the Astrodome, which was considered the eighth wonder of the world at that time. So, along with one of his teammates, he drove down to Houston because the Oilers were having open tryouts. He was feeling healthy and excited at the chance to finally get back into the groove and show people what he was capable of, especially the coaching staff on an NFL team.

The Oilers worked him out, and I get the feeling they saw his natural talent, but the forty-yard dash he ran wasn't anywhere close to his best time. The coaches were straight and told him he needed to be faster and could try again next season. My dad agreed but was devastated with himself. He knew he had an opportunity and hadn't prepared properly. Within a few months the team signed Billy "White Shoe" Johnson and gave him the number 84. Billy went on to be one of the greatest kick return men in the history of NFL.

It took nearly thirty years, but my dad's dream came true in a sense when I was signed by the Houston Texans. He was so thrilled, and one of the greatest gifts of my life was seeing the joy in his face when he heard the news. As he was my parent, I was a reflection of him, and he had played a major part in getting me to that level. And, if we needed any proof that God works in mysterious ways, I was given the number 84, the same number my dad would have worn had he became an Oiler.

My dad told me numerous times about how much he enjoyed watching me play in the NFL. I felt grateful because I sensed making the team not only made my dad proud, but also helped him with the unresolved dream he had for his own life. Researchers from Utrecht University in the Netherlands found that parents who experience unresolved disappointments from the past feel pride and fulfillment when they can bask in their children's glory. I didn't need any study to see a certain weight lifted off my father's shoulders.

The reason that I even made the NFL was because my dad *did not* force his dream on me. He showed me his love by always being supportive and present, and by providing positive affirmations instead of harsh and critical reprimands. This fueled my confidence and self-esteem and had a major impact on shaping my resolve toward challenges. He didn't have me out running drills as a preschooler and wasn't yelling at refs in any of my childhood games. He played his part in the background and allowed us to discover our own passion and talents. That is the secret to motivating people—show them the rewards, the fun, the passion, the growth instead of focusing on the results. The author Antoine de Saint-Exupéry is quoted as saying, "If you want to build a ship, don't drum up the men to gather wood, divide the work, and give orders. Instead, teach them to yearn for the vast and endless sea."

As my wife and I raise our young children and focus on their success in life, there are a few old lessons we have learned from our parents and some new ones we have learned along our parenting journey that we implement in their upbringing:

## 1. Keep it in house

Correct your child in the privacy of your household, not in front of others. I have seen parents screaming and yelling at the top of their lungs during their child's game, trying to motivate them. In reality, this tactic only embarrasses your child, makes them to freeze up, and, often, demolishes their sense of self-worth. Discipline is not releasing your anger toward your child, but it is lovingly and firmly guiding them to do better.

## 2. Don't force the dream

As a parent, it is natural to want to see your kids succeed, but what is success? Is it what you want? If my dad was the best accountant in the state and wanted that for me, it would not have been a good fit. Listen to what your kids find a passion in. Be mindful that the dream is pursued through hard work, dedication, and faith. Success is not success if it doesn't include health, good relationships, and building a strong faith in your children. Every person has their own path to their purpose, and when you focus on building the intangibles in your child, they will be set on the course to realizing their dreams, not yours.

## 3. Support your kids

Creating a strong support system for your children is vital in encouraging them to take risks and chase their dreams. Your child will learn to lead and face fear and anxiety with your support and encouragement along the way. When they begin to express a desire or interest in a hobby or skill, give them the opportunity to explore it. When it develops into a passion, keep them in that arena and support them through the wins and losses.

## 4. Acknowledge their effort

Be attentive to your child and acknowledge their efforts. By recognizing and supporting them, you are helping showcase a healthy, supportive relationship. You are still there standing when they get lit up and scored on over and over, and you are there when they hoist the trophy. You send the message that you will always be there, regardless of the score.

## 5. Quality time

Be there. And when you are there, be present. Being present in your child's life is fundamental to their growth and development. Prioritizing quality time will also help you discover what your child enjoys and see their passions up close. Putting down the phone at dinner or turning off the TV to listen shows them you are engaged and all your attention is on them. One of the greatest ways to love your child is by giving them your time and attention.

## 6. Unconditional love

Watching our children make mistakes can be painful. We spend a considerable amount of time protecting and keeping them from making mistakes while they are young, so it can be especially hard when the time comes for them to learn on their own. Teach your child that skill and they will never walk away from a challenge feeling defeated. As a parent, release your children from perfectionism and the idea that they cannot fail. Ultimately, I want my children to feel like their safest place to fail and recover is within our home.

---

In conclusion, I believe these twenty-one powerful steps will transform your mindset and propel you into the next level of your life, where you not only wish to see dreams come true but actually live them out.

Take this prepared to win mindset on your journey to accomplishing your goals and dreams. As you have read in my personal stories, the promised land can be recognized by the giants that stand in your way. Don't let that intimidate you—obstacles are necessary for you to discover what's truly on the inside of you. Each test or difficulty serves as an opportunity to discover the potential for your growth and what God has put in you to win. You are meant to win, so stay focused!

# ACKNOWLEDGMENTS

My relationship with Jesus Christ is the foundation on which my life is built. Every good thing has come through the friendship and faith I have in Christ; it is from Him that I draw strength, wisdom, and guidance for my life, relationships, and career.

To my beautiful wife and best friend, Sarah, without your love, support, guidance, and companionship my life and career wouldn't be the same. You have been a part of the writing process of this book from day one, and I am so grateful for your contributions and insight, most importantly your belief in this project. You prepare me to win in every facet of my life. I will love you forever!

To my daughters and son, Zoe, Noelle, and Jace, you mean the world to me. Being your dad is the greatest gift God has given me. I am so proud of you. I love you!

To my parents, Jerry and Shirley Moses, thank you for always believing in me and making me feel like I could accomplish anything I put my mind and heart to. Mom, your constant love and support mean everything to me. Your kindness and love for our family have made a tremendous impact on my life. Dad, you were not only a loving father but my best friend and mentor! You will always be my hero, #32. I miss you greatly. One love!

To my brothers—you are the best brothers; my wonderful brothers-in-law and sisters-in-law and my amazing nephews and nieces—thank you for your love and support.

To my extended family—my uncles, aunts, and cousins—thank you for the wonderful memories growing up and the continued love and support.

To my father and mother-in-law, Ipe and Susie Mathai, thank you for the unconditional love and support in my life and for believing in God's plan for our family.

To my pastors, Joel and Victoria Osteen, I am so grateful for you both. Your humility, kindness, and positivity are an inspiration to me, and I'm grateful for your leadership and ministry. It has had a profound impact on my family and me. To the Osteen Family—Ms. Dodie, Dr. Paul and Jennifer, Pastor Lisa and Kevin Comes, and your families, thank you for your love and friendship over the years. I'm so grateful that God brought me to Lakewood Church, it was truly a divine connection that opened the door to one of the most meaningful chapters of my life. I'm grateful for your leadership and example.

Thank you to my Lakewood Church family—what a joy it has been to be a part of a loving and supportive church community where I get to worship and serve each week. You have been a source of inspiration in my life, and I am grateful for the many friendships formed over the years.

To my friends, colleagues, teammates, coaches, and business partners in Iowa and Houston, thank you for your friendship, trust, collaboration, and partnership in my life and career. You have inspired me and supported me in ways I will always be grateful for.

To my literary agent Shannon Marven of Dupree Miller & Associates, thank you believing in this manuscript and for journeying with me through my first ever book. I am grateful for your expertise and insight.

Thank you to the team at Post Hill Press and Anthony Ziccardi for making this book come to life. The journey has been remarkable and a dream come true.